LINCOLN CHRISTIAN UNIVERSITY

"Sam Metcalf makes a compelling case for the biblical pattern of local churches and apostolic bands in dynamic partnership. The fulfillment of the Great Commission demands it. Along the way Sam illustrates these principles with stories and case studies gleaned from a lifetime of experience in world mission."

Steve Addison, author of *Pioneering Movements* and *What Jesus Started*

"This groundbreaking book challenges us to think differently and more biblically regarding local church and mission. . . . For the sake of the gospel and the kingdom, Sam helps us break out into a new and deeper understanding of the apostolic and local. We must take seriously and practically the seminal teaching of this volume."

Jerry White, international president emeritus, The Navigators

"Provocative and insightful, this book can challenge your thinking about what it means to be the church. Although you may not agree with everything, this book will help you sharpen your perspectives and strategies."

Bob Logan, author of *The Missional Journey*

"Sam Metcalf presents challenging and provocative ideas regarding the apostolic calling of the church and how this should inform the way we view and affirm apostolic organizations and structures that have often been considered 'para' church. This is a great read for those praying for gospel movements throughout the world."

Matthew Lee, director of church planting programs, Fuller Theological Seminary

"It motivated me to think about teaching church history with this vision in mind, and to keep my eye out for leaders who can fulfill this apostolic calling. This is the kind of book that will lead us into the future."

Gerald L. Sittser, professor of theology, Whitworth University, author of *Water from a Deep Well* and *A Grace Disguised*

"The book is a clarion call: it is time the western church returned to the fullness of what it means to be Christ's church on earth."

Marc T. Canner, professor of intercultu
Spokane, executive director of the Instit

"Sam Metcalf writes out of research and experience with freshness, humor and passion. The church as a whole desperately needs to catch up with what he calls the ministries of both left and right feet, in order to walk as God intended."

George Lings, director, Church Army's Research Unit of the Anglican Church, Sheffield, UK

"This is a book that has needed to be written for a long time. Now it is finally here and in your hands! What better person to write it than Sam Metcalf, who has spent his entire adult life spawning these apostolic movements of which he speaks."

Hans Finzel, president, HDLeaders, author of *The Top Ten Mistakes Leaders Make*

"This book will bring healing to those who have been hurt or alienated by the lack of understanding regarding the biblical nature of the church and the complementarity of the local church and apostolic ministries in their wholehearted pursuit of God's redemptive agenda on earth."

Iliya Majam, director, Harvest Leaders Network, Abuja, Nigeria

"Sam Metcalf has written a book some will find provocative, outside the lines and perhaps even testy, from a number of perspectives. . . . What no one will question is the intensity and passion he brings to the mission."

Herbert H. Slatery, attorney general, State of Tennessee

"Sam Metcalf has given the best definition and understanding of 'apostolic ministry' I've ever seen. . . . If embraced, missions movements and local churches around the world could be transformed."

Debbie Brink, USA senior vice president, SAT-7

"Sam Metcalf challenges our assumptions about the role of the local church, missionaries, control and accountability, and offers a biblical and historical basis to free up those with apostolic calling to do what they do best—creating new forms of church as spiritual entrepreneurs."

David Bute, director, Kreativity, Mission Impossible, Cherkassy, Ukraine

"This book by Sam Metcalf is the primer that has been missing for releasing and establishing dynamic apostolic work and 'sent' church systems that are complementary, rather than merely subservient, to the local church. . . . I already have a list of people to whom I would like to give a copy!"

Adam Atkinson, vicar, Saint Peter's Anglican Church, Bethnal Green, London

BEYOND THE LOCAL CHURCH

HOW APOSTOLIC MOVEMENTS CAN CHANGE THE WORLD

SAM METCALF

IVP Books

An imprint of InterVarsity Press
Downers Grove, Illinois

InterVarsity Press
P.O. Box 1400, Downers Grove, IL 60515-1426
ivpress.com
email@ivpress.com

©2015 by Sam Metcalf

All rights reserved. No part of this book may be reproduced in any form without written permission from InterVarsity Press.

InterVarsity Press® is the book-publishing division of InterVarsity Christian Fellowship/USA®, a movement of students and faculty active on campus at hundreds of universities, colleges and schools of nursing in the United States of America, and a member movement of the International Fellowship of Evangelical Students. For information about local and regional activities, visit intervarsity.org.

All Scripture quotations, unless otherwise indicated, are taken from THE HOLY BIBLE, NEW INTERNATIONAL VERSION®, NIV® Copyright © 1973, 1978, 1984, 2011 by Biblica, Inc.™ Used by permission. All rights reserved worldwide.

While any stories in this book are true, some names and identifying information may have been changed to protect the privacy of individuals.

The poem on pp. 149-50 is "In Celebration of Missionaries" from Psalms of My Life *by Joseph Bayly. Used by permission of the Bayly family.*

Figure 5.2 on p. 111 and excerpts from Alan Hirsch and Tim Catchim, The Permanent Revolution: Apostolic Imagination and Practice for the 21st Century Church *(San Francisco: Jossey-Bass, 2012) are reproduced with permission of John Wiley & Sons, Inc.*

Excerpts from C. Peter Wagner, The Book of Acts: A Commentary *(Bloomington, MN: Chosen Books, 2014) are used by permission of Chosen Books, a division of Baker Publishing Group.*

Published in association with the literary agency of WordServe Literary Group, Ltd., www.wordserveliterary.com.

Cover design: David Fassett
Interior design: Beth McGill
Images: birds in flight: EyeEm/Getty Images
little white church: ©sumnersgraphicsinc/iStockphoto

ISBN 978-0-8308-4436-4 (print)
ISBN 978-0-8308-9889-3 (digital)

Printed in the United States of America ♾

 As a member of the Green Press Initiative, InterVarsity Press is committed to protecting the environment and to the responsible use of natural resources. To learn more, visit greenpressinitiative.org.

Library of Congress Cataloging-in-Publication Data
Metcalf, Sam, 1952-
  Beyond the local church : how apostolic movements can change the world / Sam Metcalf.
     pages cm
  Includes bibliographical references.
  ISBN 978-0-8308-4436-4 (pbk. : alk. paper)
  1. Christianity--Societies, etc. 2. Church. I. Title.
  BR21.M48 2015
  267--dc23
                                                                                            201502699

P   20   19   18   17   16   15   14   13   12   11   10   9   8   7   6   5   4   3   2   1

Y   32   31   30   29   28   27   26   25   24   23   22   21   20   19   18   17   16   15

To all those throughout CRM

—my friends and fellow apostolic adventurers—

as we've journeyed together. It's been extraordinary.

Thank you for the ride!

130897

Contents

Foreword

by Alan Hirsch

The great Christian revolutions come not by the discovery of something that was not known before. They happen when someone takes radically something that was always there.

H. Richard Niebuhr

One of the more stimulating books I have read in recent years was *The Age of the Unthinkable* by Joshua Cooper Ramo.[1] The "unthinkable" in Ramo's view is akin to a kind of future/culture shock we experience in problematic encounters of the twenty-first century as we enter into previously uncharted waters. This is largely due to massive economic, political, environmental and social factors as they shift. Our age is highly unstable and at the edge of seismic cultural change. And yet we are entering into this revolutionary age armed with a mindset formed and suited for centuries past. The central warning of Ramo's book highlights how and why an obsolete picture of the world only serves to exacerbate, not resolve, the serious global problems we face.

As a global missionary leader, Sam Metcalf knows this. He senses

that we are ill prepared for the paradigmatic challenges of the on-
coming century. But in order to propose a way forward, Sam knows
that he has to expose the reductionist ecclesiology implied in the
inherited Western understandings of the church. He aims squarely
at the reduction of Jesus' *ecclesia* to the merely local and of its leadership to the merely pastoral. He is spot on here.

The divorce of the local church from the missionary church is a
systemic disaster to be sure. At the very roots of the twentieth
century, Roland Allen, the remarkable missionary to China, pre-
dicted that with the birth of the so-called parachurch and the missionary societies that we would "end up with a mission-less church
and a church-less mission."[2] This rupture on the NT ecclesiology
introduced an element of deep dysfunction into both the local
church and the resultant "parachurches" and undercut the possibility of movements occurring.

I have long believed that if we understand ecclesia properly
and begin to reappropriate its various levels of meaning, then
many of the problems we now face can be resolved. For instance,
our more concrete, over-localized, fairly institutionalized paradigm of church must be redefined in the much broader, more
fluid meaning used in the Bible.

The confining of the church to the simply local has had disastrous
consequences for our capacity to imagine the church as a transformative movement that can reach across vast geographic regions and
penetrate numerous cultures. The local church as we know it can
barely reach past its own internal programming, let alone transform
whole cultures and societies. And yet I believe that is what the
church is designed by Jesus to do. We have to expand our understanding of the church to that of a burgeoning apostolic movement,
not reduce it to a one-dimensional religious institution. This is the
church that is equal to the challenge of the twenty-first century.

Drawing on Ralph Winter's categories, the best thinking of missional leadership and years of experience, Sam develops a coherent and strategically useful typology of missional leadership along with the associated missional organization.

But in *Beyond the Local Church* Sam doesn't just suggest new ways of organizing. He also highlights the importance of expanding our also severely diminished understanding of ministry beyond that of the shepherd and teacher to include the generative ministries of the apostle (missional), prophet and evangelist envisaged in Ephesians 4:1-16 (APEST).

I have always felt the urgency and sheer strategic value of this neglected aspect of biblical ecclesiology and have written about it in almost every book I have published. Most recently, and in the most consistent and thorough form, I have written about it with Tim Catchim in *The Permanent Revolution.* I am completely convinced we need to first and foremost reconceive the church as a missional, or better, *apostolic*, movement. Once we embrace this more biblical paradigm of church, we will then begin to think and act like the movement we are designed to be. But if we are to re-embrace the movement form (and I can see no viable plan B for the church in the West) then we are going to have to likewise re-embrace the very forms of ministry that can generate, sustain and develop missional movements. And we can do no better than recover the world changing dynamics latent in the APEST typology. Sam has added to the needed dialogue by adding his leadership experience and intellectual heft to the conversation. I, for one, am grateful.

This is a very welcome contribution to the area of missional structures and leadership based on the thoroughly biblical APEST ministry typology that we see operative throughout the book of Acts and the early church. I hope and trust this book will help the reader rediscover the sheer potency laced throughout a genuinely missional understanding of the church.

One feels Sam's love of God, the Bible and the history and

mission of the church throughout. I trust that having read this book, and followed its counsel, we will all find ourselves more faithful to the particular work of God in our generation.

If you are one of those whose heart is stirred by this volume— and who sense a new freedom and opportunity to pursue an apostolic calling—I urge you to action. If you are so gifted and inclined, then please jump in wholeheartedly, either in the local church context *or* in the type of structures Sam advocates for so strongly. Don't stay on the sidelines. Too much is at stake!

Alan Hirsch
Author of numerous books on missional Christianity and founder of Forge Mission Training Network and Future Travelers
www.alanhirsch.org

Introduction

*The renewal of the church will come from a new
type of monasticism, which has only in common with the
old an uncompromising allegiance to the Sermon
on the Mount. It is high time men and
women banded together to do this.*

Dietrich Bonhoeffer

*Send us people with initiative. Send only Pauls and Timothys . . .
who are full of zeal, holiness and power. All others are
hindrances. If you send us ten such men the
work will be done. Quantity is nothing;
quality is what matters.*

C.T. Studd, pioneer missionary to China, India and Africa

I remember playing a game as a child in which we would bend one
knee and grab our foot behind us and then try to race—limping,
stumbling and falling over as we struggled across the grass toward
a finish line.

That's what happens when we have only one leg to stand on, or assume that somehow two left feet suffice for one of each. This balancing act is repeated throughout most of nature. Two eyes to give perspective. Two arms and two hands to provide dexterity. Two sides of our brain that operate separately, yet in tandem. All these things come in pairs because there are many things in the physical world that work best when they have balance and complementarity.

So it is when we mistakenly assume that the local church is all there is or should be when it comes to God's redemptive purposes. It's like trying to run on two left feet. The results can be as sadly hilarious as they were when I was running those races as a child, limping along on only one foot.

There is a divine, structural symmetry that we ignore to our peril. In the Protestant world, of which I am a part, the denial of the legitimacy of the other form of the church—the necessary right foot—has been far too prevalent and even the norm during the five hundred years since Martin Luther nailed his Ninety-five Theses to the Wittenberg church door.

LOOKING FOR MORE?

I grew up in a home where local church involvement was a given, and in my experience it was mostly healthy and nurturing. But from an early age, I struggled with the uneasy feeling that for me there had to be something else, something beyond that experience. When I gained exposure in my high school and university days to ministries such as Young Life, Campus Crusade (Cru), the Navigators, InterVarsity, World Vision and many more, a broader world of ministry opened up. I discovered experientially that the left foot was not enough, at least for me—and I found that discovery incredibly liberating. I suspect I would have jettisoned my faith had it not been for such involvement beyond the local church.

But while I knew and understood this intuitively, it was only years later that I discovered *why* that was the case, as I was exposed to the biblical and historical evidence that supported an understanding of the church in both its right- *and* left-footed forms. I learned that these missionary structures beyond the local church were the places where many of the people with what the Bible refers to as apostolic gifting or calling could be fulfilled. These structures were the ideal platforms where the "sent ones"—the basic meaning of the word *apostolic* in the Bible—could thrive and make their ultimate contribution to God's plans and purposes.

And I learned, contrary to what I had heard in my local church setting, that these ministries outside and beyond the local church were not aberrations. They didn't exist just because the local church was not doing what it was supposed to do. Far from it. These apostolic missionary structures existed by the design and plan of God. They were never afterthoughts.

YOU'RE NOT ALONE

What I've found, after decades of ministry in dozens of countries with hundreds of leaders, pastors and missionaries of every imaginable configuration, is that I'm not alone. I consistently engage those who have been similarly frustrated and are limping along on one foot, falsely believing that they are relegated to this state for the rest of their lives. Perhaps you are one of these. You wish there was something different to suit your gifts and calling, but when you find it, you feel guilty somehow, because it's "parachurch" and not quite legitimate. If so, this book is specifically for you.

Travis was just such a person. After university, he was part of a church plant (which failed) and then worked his way through seminary as a bartender. In retrospect, he says, he had a more authentic ministry behind the bar than in the church plant.

When we met, Travis was wondering what was next. While he was appreciative of the local church that had nurtured him in earlier years, he knew in the core of his being that the local church context somehow did not fit him. Today, in his early thirties, he leads teams of likeminded missionaries—highly committed people who, while doing life together in community, are pursuing a focused, missional vision in neighborhoods and cities worldwide. Around them, new expressions of local churches are emerging. But these teams that Travis leads are not local churches, nor do they try to be.

Throughout the Protestant world, too many of us continue to plow ahead with a self-inflicted handicap which does not fully validate or affirm those with an apostolic calling, like Travis, or the missional structures that are necessary for such men and women to flourish. Out of a noble sense of loyalty to the local church, we blindly limp along as ecclesiological cripples.

Sidelining apostolic calling and the structures necessary for its full expression is primarily a Protestant problem—the Roman Catholics and Orthodox don't struggle much with this issue. They have simply taken the biblical, historical and missiological reality of two complementary expressions of the church and institutionalized it through their religious orders. Thus they have validated a plethora of nonlocal structures that are ongoing sources of spiritual vitality and renewal for the whole body of Christ. And they have been extraordinarily effective. Despite the inevitable politics and internal jostling for power and influence over the centuries, the Catholics and the Orthodox have been quite successful in harnessing apostolic organizational dynamics and structures.

LET'S REMONK IT!

In August 1988 an editorial appeared in *Christianity Today* entitled "Remonking the Church."[1] It was a wonderful call for the reestablishment of a robust, fully-orbed expression of the church in the Protestant world, which would lead to more order-like ministries. It would also lead to more teams and communities like the ones Travis leads. It would lead to an expansion of our understanding of the church to include right- as well as left-footed expressions.

When that editorial was published, I thought it was bold and even risky for the writers. It showed a high degree of missiological insight—more than I would have anticipated at that particular time from the flagship magazine of the North American evangelical establishment.

I presently share responsibility for over five hundred people working in over eighty nations. Wherever these people are, they do one or more of three things. First, they live among unreached, unchurched or dechurched people, creating movements of the gospel where existing churches cannot or will not go. Second, they help mobilize existing churches and church leaders for mission, so that these local bodies can reach their own near neighbors and see them become obedient followers of Jesus. And third, they live incarnationally among the poor and marginalized in order to see disciples of Jesus multiplied and their communities transformed by the power and presence of Christ.

From this position, I have come to the conclusion that the essence of that editorial in *Christianity Today* was more than bold. It was prophetic. Whether it's ministry among the remaining unreached people groups of the world or regaining the momentum of the Christian movement in the postmodern West, an essential key to effectiveness is the reemergence of the apostolic structures of the church and of apostolically called people to populate them. Such a reemergence will require a shift in thinking, particularly among some religious leaders—both pastoral and denominational—about the legitimacy and essentiality of the structures needed for many with apostolic gifts to thrive. Both right and left feet are necessary.

WHO THIS BOOK IS FOR

My focus is primarily on those of us who are called by God to live and work in nonlocal church ministries, engaging those we long to become followers of Jesus. My purpose is to validate our calling: to show that our calling and the structures in which we live and work are just as anatomically essential to the mission of God as local churches, and that without us, movements would rarely ever happen. We live, day in and day out around the world, with the implications of what "church" really means to people who may be radically far away from God. For the people among whom we minister, our understanding of these truths has life-and-death consequences, and the fate of multitudes is at stake.

This is not some esoteric argument for the halls of the academy. It is my conviction that the future of the Christian movement depends on our ability to not just grasp these concepts, but to put them into action and to reengage the cultures around us with a holistic, biblical gospel. It is to live out in a contemporary setting the great truth articulated at Nicaea: "We believe in one holy, catholic *and* apostolic Church." As I hope to demonstrate in this volume, such a biblical and missional perspective is difficult, if not impossible, when we cling to a limited concept of the body of Christ that says the church in its local expression is all that's valid.

The message is simple: The creation and multiplication of structures where apostolic calling can be lived out to the fullest are critical to the mission of God and the health and vitality of the body of Christ, and are essential for movements of the good news of Jesus to occur. And the people called by God to populate these apostolic, missional structures must be validated, supported and affirmed.

THE LIMITS OF TWO LEFT FEET

Such apostolic calling and passion are rarely, if ever, fully embodied in the church in its local form. And this is not an aberration. This has always been the plan and purpose of God, demonstrated over and over again throughout redemptive history. The church in its local, cross-generational, parish, diocesan form has never been—

theologically, historically, sociologically or missiologically—designed by God to cross barriers for the sake of the expansion of his kingdom. The local church does not start movements on its own. Rather, it is supremely designed for near-neighbor missionality *and for* being a supportive base for apostolic efforts to send and equip those who do cross such barriers.

What I have written in these pages may be disturbing to some pastors and denominational officials in the Protestant world who continue to advocate a view of the church that has two left feet. Unfortunately, that's what many of us have been taught and have accepted uncritically, particularly in the West, from the days of the Reformation onward.[2] In this volume I will challenge some traditional dogmas about the nature and mission of the church, and I may upend some institutional sacred cows. I may challenge widely held assumptions to which missionaries—who should know better—often feel obligated to give lip service. I believe we must think critically about ecclesiological mantras and assumptions that, when practically applied, have contributed to impotence and retreat for the Christian movement, regardless of the context.

I am increasingly convinced that acting on these axioms is essential if the church is to regain its momentum in the West as the culture continues its slide into secular postmodernity. I believe that applying these truths is also essential if the church in the global South and the majority world is to avoid the mistakes of their brothers and sisters in the West in uncritically embracing a truncated and inadequate understanding of what the church is—an inadequacy that contributes to the ongoing stagnation and decline evident in Europe and North America.

This topic is not faddish. Rather, it is a timeless topic for anyone genuinely concerned about the state of the Christian movement in our world, and particularly in the West. It is an important topic for anyone serious about obedience to Jesus' words in Matthew 28 and the movement he started. That is because there has never been a significant submovement within the greater Christian movement that did not exemplify and utilize an apostolic structural dynamic at its very core. The Christian movement, and all of its various submovements, has advanced most effectively when it has gone forward with two different but complementary structural feet on the ground.

THE EMPEROR HAS NO CLOTHES

I want to be clear from the start. I am not anti-local church. Far from it. Rather, I am concerned by the uncritical acceptance of the understanding that the church in its local form is all there is when it comes to authentic expressions of the Christian movement, or the "big C" Church.

If we are brutally honest, we live in a context in North America that is largely disillusioned with those expressions of the local church that permeate our culture. The statistics show it.[3] Spirituality is not on the wane, but institutionalized religion and stagnant, irrelevant expressions of Christendom are in a free fall. People may be positive toward Jesus, but they want little to do with the church as they see it around them.

In North America, the fastest-growing segment of the population, categorized according to religious affiliation, are the "nones," meaning those who are done with formal religious affiliation. This includes the dechurched, who account for the largest category of unchurched people in the younger generation.[4] In my experience, one of the most effective ways to engage the nones with the reality of Jesus and his kingdom purposes is the patient, loving presence of apostolic people working through apostolic structures.

The prevailing voices in Western culture look at much of the local church and pronounce, through the media, arts, politics and education, that the emperor has no clothes. As Western culture continues to slide toward secularism, not just the messages of many of our local churches but their very fabric and structure are increasingly sidelined and out of touch. This cannot be solely attributed to an adversarial culture that is antagonistic toward what is perceived as Christian. Rather, those of us who are followers of Jesus in the Western world have brought much of this on ourselves. Despite our numbers, our wealth and our institutions, our influence continues its precipitous decline. As Alan Hirsch and Tim Catchim so astutely observe: "The U. S. church spends over $70 billion every decade on plants and resources and we are experiencing a decline in adherence and membership at an unprecedented rate."[5] They go on:

> All of the statistical indicators show serious infertility in Western Christianity, and so we too are caught in a despairing spiral of trended numerical and spiritual decline in just about every context in the Western world.... We have to acknowledge that after almost twenty centuries of Christianity in Western contexts, we have generally not seen the kind of transformation implied in the Gospel.[6]

I was in London browsing one of the ubiquitous British tabloids and an advertisement for a new health club grabbed my attention. The picture was of a magnificent gothic church sanctuary that had been turned into the swimming pool of the new spa. It was a telling image of the continuing demise of the Anglican Church in a city where more people attend a mosque than the Church of England on any given weekend. Or consider the church building, one block off the Royal Mile in Edinburgh, that is now a nightclub and lounge. To add insult to injury, the club is called *Sin*, and the logo that has replaced the stained glass window is a fallen angel descending from the heights of heaven.

The decline of the Christian movement in the West is well documented and unsurprising to honest observers.[7] Unfortunately, many of us are like the proverbial frog in the kettle. We remain in our religious bubbles, oblivious to the rapidity of change around us until it is too late. But the point is that without a restoration of apostolic function *and* the necessary apostolic structures, I believe there is little hope that the Christian movement will ever regain the initiative in the West. Until we understand, legitimize and embrace the essentiality of such apostolic gifting and structures, and free them from the limitations imposed by well-meaning local churches, local church leaders and denominational authorities, we will never be able to overcome the perceptions of irrelevance and marginalization that confront the good news of Jesus in the Western world.

THE NECESSITY OF STRUCTURE

While there are encouraging signs of renewal and reinvention, I perennially find conversations about structure strangely absent. Hence the emphasis and theme of this volume: *Apostolic vision without apostolic structure is only a dream.* I believe this has been true for every missional movement since Pentecost.

For example, structure was the distinguishing difference between the relative lack of long-term results in the ministry of George Whitfield as compared to that of John Wesley. Whitfield may have been considered the most influential voice for Christianity in the English-speaking world in the eighteenth century, but Wesley understood that a movement with structure would have a more lasting influence. It was through the "methods" of the Methodists that the power of their movement was harnessed, with results that lasted for many generations.

Examples like Whitfield and Wesley can be found in every epoch and age, every culture and people group for the past two thousand years, wherever the good news of Jesus has taken root. And in every instance where the Spirit of God is poured out on God's people *and* there is an accompanying structural dynamic, where the people of God are free to thrive in both local church expressions and apostolic church expressions, we see movements of the gospel emerge, all pointing to the powerful handiwork of God in his loving, redemptive purposes.

THE AWESOME POTENTIAL OF APOSTOLIC MOVEMENTS

I would like to see understanding, affirmation and a fresh avalanche of legitimacy for apostolic ministry and for the structures necessary for its fulfillment. If this biblical, historical and missiological paradigm could be embraced more fully, it is remarkable to imagine the spiritual forces, invigorated by the Spirit of God and the agents of heaven, that could be unleashed in our time. The type of movements this book describes could become the norm rather than the exception.

I long to see waves of individuals with apostolic gifting and apostolic passion released into the harvest fields of the world and the fresh, authentic movements that will inevitably result. I want to see apostolic people mobilized for effective ministry in local church settings *and* flooding into ministry beyond the local church, both far and near. Too many are sitting on the sidelines. The amount of untapped talent, unfulfilled gifts and underused skills is overwhelming. The waste is appalling.

And finally, I want to see and participate in movements in which millions of people, now far from God, move toward him and find ultimate freedom in unfettered commitment to Jesus. Such movements have rarely occurred—and will not be possible in the future—apart from the leadership of apostolic people and the multiplication of apostolic structures through which they are free to minister. Two left feet won't cut it. We need apostolic, missional structures to accommodate the apostolically gifted. The outcomes of the movements they will catalyze are not just heavenly, but are profoundly effectual in the here and now. The results will be deeply transformative for a world that is in great pain and ever-increasing need.

Can the rule of Jesus and the presence of his kingdom break in more broadly and deeply for us and for the generations to follow? Absolutely! But one critical and essential component of such kingdom reality is setting free those entrepreneurial pioneers of the kingdom called apostles, and invigorating the structures in which they thrive with energy and resources. The world is longing for expressions of the body of Christ that *run* on both feet! For the sake of his name and for the sake of his creation, may the King of the kingdom make it so in our day.

1

The Power of a Balanced Anatomy

The biblical genius and design for apostolic structures and movements

The mission of God is limited, because the models by which it can happen have been restricted.

George Lings

We believe in one holy, catholic and apostolic Church.

Nicene Creed

He was the pastor of a local church which had been generously supportive of several people serving around the world with Church Resource Ministries (CRM), the organization that I lead. But he was grappling with the question of where his responsibility to those people ended and where ours, as the mission entity with whom they served, began. It was a good struggle and one common to many who sincerely want to affirm and support those within their congregations whom God has set aside and called to be sent ones—

apostolic people, those who traverse social, cultural, linguistic or geographical barriers for the sake of the good news of Jesus.

As we talked over lunch, I cautiously began to lay out the distinctives, as I see them, between local churches and ministries like ours, and what I felt healthy interdependence between these two forms of church would look like. Some of that was easy because we both had a profound commitment to mission and to what God wants to do among the nations. But unfortunately, he had few categories for ministry outside, or not under the control of, the local congregation. Apostolic people and structures that operated outside of his local church were not really a legitimate part of his ministry paradigm.

The more we talked, the more the dissonance bubbled to the surface. Finally he blurted out, "I always suspected there were people like you in the missions world, but you're the first one I've ever heard openly say such things. You really think that you and what you do is as much the 'church' as what we do? Where do you get that from in the Bible?" He went on to suggest that it might be a good idea for me to get together with a respected theologian at a nearby seminary with the hope that my theology could be better informed.

This particular encounter haunted me afterward. Here was a faithful, conscientious pastor practically begging for some type of biblical justification for what I considered a healthy, balanced ecclesiology. I think he genuinely wanted to validate those from his congregation who had chosen a missional vocation, but no one—in seminary or afterward—had ever given him a cogent rationale for such a structure.

THE TWO-STRUCTURE PARADIGM

During the latter half of the twentieth century, Ralph Winter was one of the iconic giants of the mission world. After earning degrees from Cal Tech, Columbia, Cornell and Princeton, he and his wife,

Roberta, cut their teeth as missionaries in Guatemala, where they pioneered TEE (Theological Education by Extension), a concept which has been emulated around the world in the years since.

After a decade in Guatemala, Winter became one of the core of eminent missiologists recruited by Donald McGavran at Fuller Theological Seminary, where Winter would directly influence over one thousand missionaries, particularly through his ground-breaking course "The History of the Christian Movement." He went on to found a number of organizations, including the U. S. Center for World Mission, which spearheaded the concept of unreached people groups and has had a far-reaching influence on global mis-sionary priorities that continues to this day.

One of Winter's most important contributions to missiology was a seminal article first drafted in 1973, titled "The Two Structures of God's Redemptive Mission."[1] In this broad historical overview, Winter outlines—as only he could do—the grand themes of God's redemptive activity, and pulls all the pieces together in a way that makes sense of centuries of missionary history. It is the best his-torical treatment of a fully-orbed missional ecclesiology I've ever encountered. It explains how the design of God, from the time of the New Testament forward, has been to work through the local church *and* the church in its missionary form.

When I was at Fuller for graduate studies and came across Win-ter's article, I was astonished. No one had ever explained any of this to me. I'd never heard it before. It was as if the lights all came on, and I was granted a license of legitimacy for ministry that I had never previously experienced.

Winter makes the case that God has chosen to work throughout all of history through two primary redemptive structures. Winter gave these two structures anthropological titles. He labeled the church in its local, parish, diocesan form (what I have referred to as the left foot) a *modality,* and he labeled the church in its task-oriented, missionary, sent form a *sodality* (what I have called the right foot). Both are the church. Both are necessary.

These terms are understood and used in Roman Catholic circles and are occasionally used by Protestants too, such as Yale historian Kenneth Scott Latourette in his landmark work *The History of Christianity*.[2] But for the most part, no one can seem to remember which one is which, if they know of them at all. In this book we're using practical analogies, like left and right feet, to help distinguish these complementary parts of church anatomy.

While there are many implications that can be drawn from Winter's article, I believe three are particularly profound.

1. The church in its apostolic, missionary form is just as equally "church" as the church in its local, parish form. God never designed or intended either to do the work of the other.

2. The evidence from history is abundant that whenever these two structures work cooperatively and interdependently, the Christian movement thrives and moves forward. When one structure dominates or attempts to control the other, the movement suffers.

3. Apostolic leaders thrive best in structures uniquely designed for the fulfillment of their calling, and these leaders must have access to such structures in order to reach their God-given potential. When pastoral or denominational leaders mistakenly assume that such apostolic structures have no validity or are subject to their control, everyone loses.

COMPARING MODALITIES AND SODALITIES

The following chart is a helpful way to compare and contrast these two expressions of the church. While there are right-footed structures that are not apostolic (described in chapter five), my interest here and throughout this book is in those structures that *are* apostolic in nature, where apostolic gifting flourishes.

Table 1.1

Left Foot Structures (Modalities)	Right Foot Structures (Sodalities)
The church local	The church mobile
Diocesan, parish form	Missionary form
Structured primarily for nurture, care	Task-oriented, mobile, flexible, lean
Conserves new ground	Takes new ground, crosses barriers
"First decision" people	"Second decision" people
Ministry generalists	Ministry specialists
Multi-tasks	Narrow focus
Inclusive	Exclusive
Pastors and teachers thrive	Apostolic leaders thrive
Resources for sodalities	Creates modalities and new sodalities
Connectional	Can be trans-denominational
Occasionally multiplies	Expansionistic
Five generation life cycle	Extended generational life cycle
Primarily near neighbor missionality (E-0)[3]	Cross-culturally capable (E-1 thru E-3)
Builds, establishes and preserves	Inherently entrepreneurial

A variety of analogies—besides left and right feet—can help illustrate the distinction between these two structures. One simple way to see it is to consider the contrast between *settlers* and *pioneers*. Pioneers go somewhere. They explore new territory. They cross barriers in their efforts. Pioneers imagine what could be and are motivated by the new and unknown. This idea is captured in the famous introductory lines to every episode of *Star Trek*:

> *Space: The final frontier. These are the voyages of the starship* Enterprise. *Its five-year mission: To explore strange new worlds; to seek out new life and new civilizations; to boldly go where no man has gone before.*

Settlers, on the other hand, are those who conserve the fruit of exploration. They establish. They put down roots and build. They ensure that what has been accomplished is preserved for themselves and for future generations.

The values and mindsets of pioneers and settlers are quite different. Inevitably, they hold different values that can conflict. As George Lings says, "To the adventurous the word settler is as attractive as mud. To the systems person, pioneers are a nightmare."[4]

Each function calls for different abilities and different skill sets. Each calls for a different structure in which such abilities and skill sets can be effectively lived out. But both are valid. Both are important. Both are necessary.

The two structures distinction can be seen in an array of other areas of life. There is a difference between a classic entrepreneur who starts a business and the business manager who builds and maintains it. There is a difference between a pioneering medical researcher and a family doctor. There is a difference between a soldier who serves in Special Forces and one who serves in the regular army. Throughout most human endeavors there are distinctions between specialists and generalists and social structures that uniquely accommodate both. It is no different for the church—the universal earthly expression of those people committed to Jesus.

I wish there were a better vocabulary for explaining the distinction between *sodality* and *modality*. Others have tried various terms, but they really haven't stuck: sent church versus gathered church; pioneers versus settlers; specialists versus generalists, etc. But in our era and for those immersed in the missional task of the Christian movement, Winter brought clarity to these foundational concepts. George Lings writes:

> I resisted the language for years, because I did not understand it and found it opaque. The words conveyed almost nothing to me, except my sense of incomprehension. Having been enlightened, they are now a central part of my understanding of mission and church and I deeply regret that the terms are not more accessible. I have thought for some years about how they could be improved, and am open to offers, but all alternatives put so far by others seem only partial or even a step back.[5]

Ralph Winter's "Two Structures" article is primarily an argument from history. He does not devote much time to an exegetical or biblical justification for the distinction between these two God-ordained structures. He does little to extract the paradigm—and particularly the legitimacy of the apostolic structure—from Scripture.

I think that is understandable, because to the Jewish mind of both the Old Testament and the early stages of the Christian era, such structures would have been givens. There would be little need to justify their existence. But that is no longer the case in our day, and it is particularly not the prevailing worldview within Protestantism. So can we show some biblical justification for this missiological paradigm? Can I satisfactorily answer the question my pastor friend asked in the conversation at the beginning of this chapter? The answer is an unequivocal *yes*.

THE OLD TESTAMENT EVIDENCE

While the New Testament provides more fertile ground for understanding these concepts, there are examples of functional equivalents of apostolic, missionary structures woven throughout the Old Testament and the intertestamental period. Granted, they may be more implicit than explicit, but they are not obscure.

An early example in the Old Testament of individuals operating outside the religious establishment is the Nazirites. These were men or women who voluntarily took vows as an indication of being separated or consecrated as holy to God (Numbers 6:8). In the Halakha (the Jewish law) there is a rich tradition regarding Nazirites, and there are sixteen uses of the Hebrew word *nazir* in the Hebrew Bible. There were actually grades or levels of Nazirites and some variation in what it meant to be a Nazirite in different times. We find examples of Nazirite vows in Judges 13:5 (Samson) and 1 Samuel 1:11 (Samuel). They are also mentioned in Amos 2:11-12.

Nazirites appear in the writings of Josephus and the rabbi Gamaliel, and are referred to in 1 Maccabees 3:49. In modern Hebrew, the word *nazir* is used for monks—whether Christian, Buddhist or other non-Jewish religious expressions—as those who have been set aside for specific, holy purposes. Luke 1:13-15 suggests that John the Baptist was designated a Nazirite from birth.

Another example of a structure that accommodated such set-aside people in the Old Testament is the schools or bands of prophets started by the prophet Samuel and described in 1 Samuel 19:19-20. While prophets walked an unpopular road, the structure for living out their prophetic calling and apprenticing other prophets flourished in the days of Samuel, Elijah and Elisha, and throughout the Old Testament.

These "schools" were bands of men who lived together for instruction, worship, training and service (1 Samuel 10:2-11; 19:19-20; 1 Kings 18:4; 22:6; 2 Kings 2:3-5; 4:38; 6:1). Some commentators actually refer to these as prophetic "orders," and their influence was felt from the time of Samuel through the Babylonian exile. There is reference to these bands living in Ramah, Bethel, Gilgal, Jericho, Carmel and Samaria, where it is inferred they resided in their own buildings with their own clear sense of community and mission. There was study, worship and tasks for others and for God, all overseen by defined leadership (Samuel, Elijah and Elisha, for example). They were largely dependent on the charity of the Hebrew people for support.[6]

During the intertestamental period, the Essenes (ca. 150 BC–AD 68) were another example of a Jewish sodality structure. They practiced communal life, asceticism, voluntary poverty and abstinence from worldly pleasures, and they were committed to piety and expressions of charity and benevolence. They are best known to us today as those who produced—or at least preserved—the Dead Sea Scrolls. John the Baptist was probably influenced by the Essenes and their values, as they lived near the sites along the Jordan River where John offered baptism for repentance.

This pattern of Jewish structures continued during the intertestamental period and into the first century AD. Johannes Blauw, in *The Missionary Nature of the Church*, has a brief but fascinating chapter on missionary activity among the Jews—the "proselytizing movement" in which bands of committed Jews travelled throughout the Roman Empire to find converts.[7] Winter also refers to them:

> Very few Christians, casually reading the New Testament (and with only the New Testament available to them), would surmise the degree to which there had been Jewish evangelists who went before Paul all over the Empire—a movement that began 100 years before Christ. Some of these were the people whom Jesus himself described as "traversing land and sea to make a single proselyte." Saul followed their path; later, as Paul he built on their efforts and went beyond them with the new gospel he preached.[8]

These Jewish structures were called *khevra*, which is a Hebrew word for a voluntary association or actual mission structures. By New Testament times this included Pharisees, Essenes and Sadducees. F. F. Bruce called them "brotherhoods" and Alfred Edersheim says that the "Pharisees were an 'order,' and a 'fraternity.'"[9] Robert Blinco provides an extensive discussion of the Jewish background of these structures and is a superb source of additional documentation about the relationship between synagogues and the Jewish *khevrot*.[10]

All of these movements—Nazirites, the schools or bands of prophets, the Essenes and Jewish proselytizers—embody characteristics that we see later expressed, to one degree or another, not just in the missionary impetus of the early apostolic bands in the book of Acts, but also in the monastic missionary movements of early Christianity.

THE NEW TESTAMENT EVIDENCE

One could make a case that Jesus and his traveling band of disciples were another example of such a structure. His method of ministry and apprenticing others was a common religious form outside of the religious establishment and the temple/synagogue tradition. However, the most overt evidence of apostolic structures in the New Testament is found in the book of Acts and throughout the subsequent writings of Paul the "apostle" and others who were part of his missionary bands. The first record of such post-Pentecost ministry is Acts 13:

> The Holy Spirit said, "Set apart for me Barnabas and Saul for the work to which I have called them." So after they had fasted and prayed, they placed their hands on them and sent them off. (Acts 13:2-3)

And it's not just Barnabas and Saul who are part of this effort. The mention of John Mark in verse 5 and Paul's "companions" in verse 13 implies there were other participants.

So what is really going on here? Is this an example of the church in its local form "sending" people into ministry that will cross cultural and geographical barriers? And what is the real relationship between the church in Antioch and this newly formed missionary band? Is this really an example of Paul and Barnabas in some sense being authoritatively commissioned by the Antioch church? Two things need to be said that shed important light on the legitimacy of such apostolic, missionary structures and their relationship with the local church body from this passage.

Paul and his band were "released," not sent. Let's get the exegesis right. First, the operative agent here is the Holy Spirit, not the local church or any other human entity. Second, what those around Paul and Barnabas did was recognize the Spirit's activity and sovereign choice, and they responded by *releasing* Paul and Barnabas. As C. Peter Wagner writes in his commentary on the book of Acts,

> Some scholars point out an interesting use of two Greek words for "to send" in this passage. Obviously, the chief sending agent

was the Holy Spirit, and the Greek verb in the sentence "So, being sent out by the Holy Spirit" is *pempo*, which is usually a more proactive kind of sending or dispatching. The "send" in "they *sent* them away" is from the Greek word *apoluo*, which frequently means releasing something that has its own inherent source of energy. Thus it could be said that "they released them." Certainly here we have a combination of the two kinds of sending and spiritual power for missionary activity coming ultimately from the Holy Spirit.[11]

There is no exegetical evidence to support the oft-cited perspective that the Antioch church somehow exercised authority in sending Paul and Barnabas. Of the sixty times the verb *apoluō* is used in the New Testament, only once (in Acts 15:30—and it's unclear in that passage) is the concept anywhere near a sending function with any sense of authority on the part of the sender. That's just not the way the word is used, and to imply differently is to read into the text something that is simply not there.[12] Paul and Barnabas were, rather, "released from their local responsibilities and allowed to return to the kind of work that had brought them to Antioch in the first place."[13]

There is no New Testament text that describes a local congregation as "sending" or "commissioning" people for long-term pioneer missionary service to plant churches where there were none. This does not mean that it is contrary to Scripture for a church to do so today; it only means that there is no biblical text that directly supports the use of that terminology.[14] As Robert Blincoe writes, "Appealing to Acts 13:1-3 to secure a biblical basis for today's church assessment and funding and oversight of missionaries seems to be treading on thin ice."

There are no examples anywhere in Scripture of local church governance of the missionary undertaking. One passage that could be cited—and it's a stretch—is Galatians 2:11-14, and that particular example is negative. It's not a precedent I would cite if I were a local church that believes in tighter control of apostolic, sent people.[15]

Those who did the releasing may not actually have been the local church leaders. An interesting argument could be made that those who laid their hands on Paul and Barnabas were actually other apostolic leaders—not unlike Paul and Barnabas—who were releasing some of their own for a new assignment. We need to consider the possibility that none of these were from Antioch or residents there long-term. And in an environment where the local church consisted of multiple house churches, none of these were pastors or elders of these groups. Acts 13:1 implies that prophets and teachers were not also called "elders." It's possible that these prophets and teachers were what we often find when people move crossculturally and minister alongside burgeoning or existing church expressions, that is, missionaries.

So it's quite possible that three of Paul's team are—by the process of the laying-on of hands—setting aside two of their own to be sent. As Peter Wagner writes:

> Who laid on hands? As far as the text is concerned, the other three would have laid hands on Barnabas and Saul. Whether any others from either the sodality or the modality would have been invited to participate is a matter of conjecture. Most students of Acts think the church in general would have played some role. In all probability it did, but it should be seen as a secondary, not a primary, role.[16]

Elsewhere, Wagner explains,

> Keep in mind that Barnabas and Paul did not first become missionaries at this point. They were already missionaries, simply being reassigned. The process of hearing from God

and reassigning the missionaries accordingly took place within what missiologists call the "sodality," or the CCM [Cyprus and Cyrene Mission] mission agency, not the "modality," or the Antioch church as such. . . . It is not an attempt to demote the local church, but only to point out that . . . when it comes to particulars of mission strategy . . . God more often speaks to apostolic teams than to home congregations.[17]

I realize that Wagner's view is speculative, but there is nothing in the text that would prevent it. Regardless, the belief that Acts 13 somehow demonstrates that local congregations should have authority over the sending and ongoing governance of missionary teams is simply unsupportable by the text. As Craig Van Gelder notes, "once Barnabas and Paul were sent out by the Antioch church, they were basically on their own. They were neither under the control of Antioch in decision making, nor were they dependent upon Antioch for financial support."[18]

So from Acts 13 through Paul's three missionary journeys, we see the powerful utility and effectiveness of these apostolic bands. They were flexible and never static. They were mobile. They were task oriented. People came and went, such as Luke, Titus, Timothy and John Mark. There was communication between the teams. At least thirty or more individuals are specifically named at one point or another in the New Testament as participants in this Cyprus and Cyrene Mission.

ABERRATIONS OR EQUALS?

There are significant implications if in fact Wagner and the missiological commentators who agree with him are correct in their understanding of these passages and the subsequent ministry activity of Paul and his missionary band(s). This speaks directly to the relationship between the church in its missionary form and the church in its local form.

First, these apostolic bands were not aberrations. As Charles Mellis states:

> Another interesting feature is that these teams are never described in a didactic way. Yet the abundant evidence of their activity shows how thoroughly they were accepted as a valid and vital structure of the church, the Body of Christ. But is it really so strange that Paul, who was responsible for so much of the New Testament's formal teaching, would not *describe* the missionary band? After all, he was *demonstrating* its function at every step. And he also demonstrated his relationship to the local nurturing fellowships that he and his teams planted—by the way he wrote to these congregations in certain cities.[19]

The absence of an explicit description of these apostolic bands as "church" in the post-Gospel writings does not preclude the description from being legitimately applied to Paul and his apostolic band(s). It is not only the church "local" that is church. There is simply no textual reason to prohibit all of the same biblical and essential descriptors of "church" that are applied to geographically local, congregational entities from being equally applied to mobile, apostolic structures.

Second, the primary structure used in the New Testament for missionary efforts—meaning the crossing of cultural, linguistic or geographical barriers for the sake of mission—is not the church in its local form. Rather, it is the church in its missionary form, full of apostolic people. That form is not by accident or default, but by the design and providence of God. As Wagner says:

> The predominant structure for the extension of the Kingdom of God into new mission frontiers has been the sodality, not the modality. Each has its essential place in the Kingdom, but for cross cultural missions God seems to have favored the

sodality. This is why I believe it is important to understand that in Antioch the Holy Spirit evidently spoke to the sodality (the CCM) instead of the modality (the Antioch church) to "separate to Me Barnabas and Saul for the work to which I have called them" (13:2). That is the reason why I think it is inaccurate to say, as many do, that Paul and Barnabas were sent out by the church at Antioch.[20]

CONTROL AND ACCOUNTABILITY

Implicit in this conversation is the question of control and accountability. I sometimes hear pastors and denominational leaders say that they—and their local church or denominational structure—should be the ones in control of apostolic leaders and their ministry efforts. But that is a difficult position to justify from Scripture.

First, there is no evidence that Antioch, or any other local congregation, played a controlling role in the function and decisions of Paul and his apostolic teams. None. In fact, the opposite was more often the case. When Paul recruited personnel, he didn't submit their resumes to the local churches or seek their approval. He may have sought their advice (as with Timothy in Acts 16:2), but there is no evidence of control. When Paul made strategic decisions, such as launching off into Macedonia or going to Rome, he got his marching orders directly from the Holy Spirit. While he did report his activity to local churches (Acts 14:26-28) and send regular letters and messengers (which were the social media of the times), there is no evidence that his efforts or the efforts of his missionary bands were under the authority or control of local congregations. In fact, the reverse is actually more accurate. Most of the post-Gospel New Testament writings are actually letters from apostolic people operating in apostolic structures to local church people on how to live, minister and function. Mellis writes:

> There is no evidence that the life of the missionary band was "rooted" in or controlled by this church. Nor is there any hint of a financially supportive relationship. On the contrary, the evidence points to the fact that the bands had a life of their own, and threw off shoots which became the planted communities of believers. Green (following Harnack) calls attention to this distinction as it carried over into the second century. . . . He speaks of a division of "peripatetic Christian leaders which was extremely ancient, and probably modeled on Jewish precedent; they stand out in sharp contrast to the settled ministry of bishops, presbyters and deacons. . . . Both types of ministry are found side by side in the *Didache* and *Hermas.* . . . The roving ministry was . . . not elected by the churches, like the settled ministry." We have here a clearly autonomous structure.[21]

Theologian Arthur Glasser sums it up well:

> There is no indication that the apostolic missionary team was either directed by or accountable to the Christians in Antioch. . . . We state this without qualification, even though upon returning from their first journey, Paul and Barnabas "gathered the church together and declared all that God had done with them."[22]

Autonomy does not mean a lack of collegiality or reciprocity. As we will see in coming chapters, movements actually occur and are sustained when there is a healthy sense of interdependence between local and apostolic expressions of the church.

However, a fair question about this noncontrolling relationship can be raised regarding Paul's relationship with the Jerusalem council. Perhaps there was no control exercised by local congregations, but what about the higher authority of this body? I agree with Charles Mellis when he writes,

> The scriptural material is extremely skimpy regarding the connection between the missionary bands and any "originating" or "sending" fellowships. We'd be on shaky ground to place the Jerusalem church in such a category. Their principle linkage with the missionary bands seems to be an endless asking of nit-picking doctrinal questions (Acts 11:2-3; 15:1, 5; etc.). The tendency became so strong that it once caused Peter to sacrifice his principles (Galatians 2:12, 13). (I imagine that every mission leader reading this will get an immediate mental picture of one or more constituency churches that he feels threatened by!) This trend continued to the point where James and the elders had to warn Paul, when he arrived in Jerusalem for his last visit, about the thousands of Jewish believers there, "all zealous for the law," who had believed some distorted rumors about his attitude toward the law. . . . The growingly inbred, law-fencing Jerusalem church is hardly a model of a mission-minded church possessing a universal message for all mankind.[23]

ENCOUNTER IN EASTERN EUROPE

Shortly after the fall of communism, I was sitting with a few of our CRM staff members in a restaurant in Budapest, Hungary. While we had engaged in itinerant, covert ministry throughout the Eastern Bloc during the bleak years before communism crumbled, we had some visionary pioneers in Hungary who were living and working "under the radar" during the difficult days of totalitarianism.

I was enjoying my coffee and the conversation when a woman approached me and introduced herself. She was another expatriate. In those days, being "recognized" in that part of the world was not something to be desired. However, she somehow recognized me—maybe because of the company I was keeping—and just wanted to say "thank you" for a recent article I had written in the *Evangelical Missions Quarterly*. The article, "When Local Churches Act Like Agencies," described in practical detail what happens when local churches assume they are capable of major apostolic ministry on their own.[24]

It turned out that this woman and her family were serving with another missions organization in Eastern Europe. She wanted me to know that the article had strongly resonated with her and her husband. It put into words what they and many other missionaries knew and felt but were hesitant to say, for fear of offending pastors and supporting churches in the United States—in particular, for fear of offending the people in those churches who controlled the purse strings. But for her, the article was liberating. It legitimized what they knew to be true about their calling. It gave them validation. They were *not* an aberration.

A fully orbed, biblical ecclesiology understands that the church can be expressed in two legitimate, autonomous but interdependent structural expressions, both necessary for the health and vitality of the overall Christian movement. Both the left foot and the right foot are absolutely needed. And these two structures—the church local and the church sent, the parish structure and the missionary structure—can be found functionally throughout the Old and New Testaments, and can be clearly justified from the pages of Scripture. But in addition to Scripture, there is the overwhelming testimony of the past two thousand years of history, to which we now turn.

2

Limping or Leaping Through Time

The encouragement of apostolic
missionality in history

*To root your consciousness in the gospel and the Scriptures;
to help you experience the presence of the triune God and
an empowered life; to help you discover and fulfill
your vocation; and to give you experience
in ministry with seekers.*

George G. Hunter III, *The Celtic Way of Evangelism*

*A theology which asserts that only the organized
Church should be involved in mission, that theology
has a very serious quarrel with history.*

Paul Pierson, *The Dynamics of Christian Mission*

The island of Iona is a windswept, barren outcrop off the Western coast of Scotland. On its shores in AD 563, the Irish monk Columba arrived with twelve companions and founded an abbey. The abbey of Iona was to become their missionary base, from which they would spread the gospel among the Picts, then the inhabitants of present-day Scotland, and beyond. Those trained at Iona would eventually go as far as Germany, Switzerland and the European lands in between as missionary ambassadors, proclaiming and living out the good news of Jesus.

St. Columba and the apostolic bands that Iona spawned were but one expression of the great Celtic missionary movement, begun with St. Patrick in the previous century, which changed the course of European history and produced a movement of authentic Christianity that lasted for over a thousand years. It was a movement that demonstrated the synergistic dynamic between apostolic structures—like Columba and his companions—and the countless local parish churches that resulted and sprang up around these Celtic bands wherever they went, preserving the labor of these pioneering spiritual entrepreneurs.

The transformative impact of this movement was so significant that historians of all stripes allude to its unquestionable contribution in the development of the Western world. Ancient texts such as Muirchú's *Life of St. Patrick* and Adomnán of Iona's *Life of St. Columba* are extraordinary firsthand accounts of these leaders and the movements they inspired. In our day, Thomas Cahill's *How the Irish Saved Civilization* and George Hunter's *The Celtic Way of Evangelism* are fascinating historical studies of the Celtic movement and how its dynamics are particularly applicable to the postmodernity of the present-day West.[1]

I've stood on that island and seen the restored Iona Abbey, in awe of the magnitude of the vision and accomplishment of Columba and his band. It is a fascinating and inspiring account of the power and effectiveness of apostolic, missionary structures to produce movements that have a massive transformative effect on the world around them.

AFTER THE BOOK OF ACTS

There is no way to completely catalog the vast expanse of church history and its countless examples of apostolic movements, which began with some of the original followers of Jesus. The apostolic tradition began early with some of the original followers of Jesus. The martyrdom of Matthew was the spark that grew into the flame of a movement among the cannibals on the Black Sea; Thomas, the doubting one, reached as far as India; and Andrew saw the Christian movement flourish among "barbarians" of Syria and Parthia.

One of the classic works that gets closest to doing this topic justice is Yale historian Kenneth Scott Latourette's *The History of Christianity*. It is one of the most comprehensive overviews I've ever read. Unlike many church histories—which can be as exciting as eating sawdust—Latourette covers in 1,500 pages the structural dynamics of the expansion (and retraction) of the Christian movement, both in the East and the Western world. "The Apostolic Through the Ages" is an online summary—drawn primarily from Latourette—that highlights apostolic leaders and movements spanning the breadth of the two millennia since Pentecost.[2] I am sure there is much that has been left out and what is recorded in this summary is only the tip of the iceberg, but we can gather from it a sense of the vast potential of apostolic ministry and apostolic people when unleashed.

THE MISSIONAL VISION OF RELIGIOUS ORDERS

From the time of the apostolic bands described in Acts until Constantine and the Edict of Milan three hundred years later, apostolic teams were a robust means by which the gospel permeated the Roman Empire. Two very distinct structures emerged—the monastery and the diocese. In the days of the early church, these may have looked like traveling missionary bands and "Christian synagogues." Both were essential to the health and the expansion of the overall Christian movement. But after waves of persecution and the inevitable drift of local parish expressions toward stability, the dynamic in the apostolic structures began to formalize, particularly after the institutionalization of the Christian movement during the time of Constantine. As Winter explains in "The Two Structures," sodalities may have evolved into different *forms* by AD 350, but they were functionally the same as their early incarnations. In some respects, the formalization and growth of these apostolic structures was an antidote to the cultural Christianity (or nominalism) that inevitably resulted from Constantine's establishmentarianism.

What we can say with confidence is that the primary engine of spiritual vigor and missional vision within Roman Catholicism throughout its long history has been the religious orders: the Benedictines, Dominicans, Franciscans, Jesuits, Missionaries of Charity, etc. The orders, which are difficult to accurately number, have been, and remain to this day, the backbone of the Catholic Church.

The best estimates put the worldwide number of women in Catholic orders close to 713,000 and the number of men at slightly less than 200,000. The *Statistical Yearbook of the Church* put the total number of Catholic adherents worldwide at about 1.23 billion at the end of 2012.[3] That means that those committed to religious orders number only about one tenth of one percent of all Catholics!

The phenomenal impact of such a small number of people is amazing. The influence of the people within these orders far exceeds their numbers. They accomplish remarkable results with few people and resources in comparison to the entire Catholic Church. The facts are:

- Most renewal has flowed historically from the orders into the modalic, diocesan structures of the Roman Catholic Church.

- Throughout history, about fifty percent of the popes have come from outside the ecclesiological hierarchy, meaning they came from the religious orders. Popes from the orders have often

brought a sweeping breath of fresh air and renewal to stodgy, ossified institutions. The present pope, Pope Francis (a Jesuit), is a
striking example.

- The historical expansion of the Catholic Church is due almost
  entirely to the evangelistic and proselytizing efforts of the missionary orders.

While all orders are sodalities, not all the sodalities within the
Catholic Church are orders, and fewer still are apostolic orders.
That is true of the Catholic Church and of non-Catholic orders as
well. Orders, by definition, are a particular subset of the vast array
of sodalities the Catholic Church has so effectively employed
throughout the centuries. (More about this in chapter four.)

So what can we learn from the Catholics?

1. Sodality structures, and particularly those that are apostolic in
   nature, are essential and integral to the health and life of the
   whole church. There is nothing "para" about them.

2. Protecting and insulating apostolic people and apostolic structures
   from the control of modalities—everything from the occasional
   ecclesiological bureaucrat to the demands of a local parish priest—
   is essential to maintaining the integrity of the apostolic function.

3. Those who are called to apostolic ministry lived out in apostolic
   structures are most often "second decision" people, meaning
   they make a deliberate *vocational* choice to join an order, a
   mission organization or some form of ministry *apart from* the
   local church. They choose to throw in their lot with others with
   similar vocational calling, and what is required of them is a
   greater degree of commitment, sacrifice and often spirituality
   than is expected of those who make "first decision" commitments at the level of the local church. (More about first and
   second decision distinctives in the coming chapters.)

THE GREAT OMISSION

One of the more troubling aspects of the Protestant Reformation was its response to these Catholic structures. In their reaction against many things Catholic, the Reformers unfortunately threw good and necessary things overboard in their reaction to the bad. They rejected structures that had lent the Catholic Church vigor over many centuries, and to which some of the Reformers, like Luther, had previously belonged. What resulted was a functionally truncated ecclesiology that hampered Protestants' ability to live out the *missio Dei*—the mission of God—in its totality and has had detrimental effects residual in the present day. As Winter writes:

> This omission, in my evaluation, represents the greatest error of the Reformation and the greatest weakness of the resulting Protestant tradition. . . . Failing to exploit the power of the sodality, the Protestants had no mechanism for missions for almost three hundred years, until William Carey . . . proposed "the use of means for the conversion of the heathen." His key word *means* refers specifically to the need for a sodality, for the organized by non-ecclesiastical initiative of the warmhearted.[4]

With some humor, Ken Mulholland writes that soon after Luther "tacked his Ninety-five Theses to the church door at Wittenberg," there came

> a tremendous explosion of missionary expansion in the wake of the Reformation, as missionaries almost immediately began to go to the ends of the earth. Correct? Wrong. William Carey did not launch the modern Protestant missionary movement until 275 years after the Reformation began. Virtually no Protestant missionary activity took place between 1517 and 1792. Yet those years constituted the golden age of Roman Catholic missions.[5]

At the same time, I want to be careful not to paint a naive picture of medieval sodalities. There were some good reasons why the Reformers reacted so strongly against them—their corruption and greed are well-documented. But as Bruce Demarest states: "The Reformers and we their evangelical descendants, acting in reaction to medieval Rome, threw out a great deal of spiritual wisdom, insight, and important practices, along with the doctrinal and ecclesiological bathwater."[6]

The Reformers' lack of missionary enterprise could be fairly referred to as "the Great Omission." It was a period largely void of significant missionary efforts, and the health and expansion of the Christian movement suffered. To be fair, there were a few notable bright spots in this period of history, such as Huguenots going to Brazil in 1556 and Nicolaus von Zinzendorf and the Moravian movement of the early eighteenth century,[7] but Protestants largely ignored the importance of sodality structures until the late eighteenth century and the emergence of what has been labeled the "modern missionary movement"—with Englishman William Carey being the primary catalyst. Before Carey—with a few exceptions—it was a dry time for Protestant missional activity.

> One of Martin Luther's blind spots was that he reacted so strongly against the corrupt aspects of the monastic movement (he belonged to the Augustinian Order) that he failed to appreciate what they were doing well. It did not occur to him to reform Catholic *missions* while he was reforming the Catholic *church.* So the Protestant Reformation movement ended up all congregational structure and no mission structure. There is no doubt that Luther himself desired that the gospel should be carried throughout the whole earth. Luther sharpened the missionary *message,* but with all his brilliance he never came clear on *missionary structures.*[8]

When Protestants missionary efforts did ramp up, well after the Reformation, their missionary structures were in typical Protestant fashion, true to stereotypical Protestant organizational culture: chaotic, decentralized and highly entrepreneurial. More was done out of missional intuition and passion than solid ecclesiological understanding.

While sorely lacking in the discipline, historicity and hierarchical structure of Catholic orders, these countless Protestant sodality structures—and the apostolic, missionary enterprises among them—have nevertheless had an enormous effect around the world over the past three centuries. For all its shortcomings, God has used the Protestant missionary movement, and the many committed apostolic people who have labored in it, in incredible ways. It has been one of the primary forces—if not the primary force—in the emergence of the Christian movement as a truly global phenomenon for the first time in human history.

PROTESTANTS GET BACK IN THE GAME

Starting with Carey, Protestants began to multiply sodalities, particularly apostolic missionary expressions, with enthusiasm. For the next three hundred years, wave after wave of Protestant structures emerged, spawning and contributing to new movements.

When Henry VIII of England separated from the Catholic Church in 1534, he subsequently dissolved the Catholic religious orders throughout England. The Anglicans suffered through the years of the Great Omission but eventually experienced a revival of religious orders, particularly in the mid-nineteenth century. These orders were often true to their Catholic roots, following Augustinian, Benedictine, Carmelite and Franciscan rules. Anglican religious orders for women are renowned for their holistic, sacrificial ministry. The Anglicans also reinvented and pioneered their own apostolic structures, such as the Church Missionary Society (1799) and the Church Army (1882).

In the eighteenth and nineteenth centuries Britain was a wellspring of innovative apostolic initiatives and the corresponding structures to facilitate them. In 1878 William and Catherine Booth founded the Salvation Army, which grew into a ministry that has a worldwide reach and reputation that extends to the present day. The YMCA, begun in 1844 in the midst of the despair of industrialized London, grew to have a global missionary impact. For example, Oswald Chambers, author of *My Utmost for His Highest*—one of the most widely read devotionals in the English language—was serving with the YMCA in Cairo, Egypt, when he died, and many of the entries in his classic devotional were written during his missionary years in North Africa.

I've lived in the London borough of Islington. Close to our flat was the imposing stone façade of the building that once housed the China Inland Mission, the missionary structure founded by Hudson Taylor. Nearby is the footprint of the Mildmay Center, where thousands gathered for missionary conferences in the mid-nineteenth century and where hundreds were trained and sent as missionaries around the world. All of this is within a two-block radius. Such historic settings abound in London, and the British legacy of creating and launching apostolic missionary expressions is truly astounding. It makes it all the more tragic to see how fast and far that apostolic fervor has declined in post–World War II Britain.

In post–World War II North America there was a burst of activity in the creation and multiplication of apostolic structures. Youth With A Mission, Campus Crusade for Christ (Cru), the Navigators, World Vision, Youth for Christ and Young Life are some of the more prominent—and there were many, many more. A variety of factors contributed to this sudden profusion of sodality structures: the great social upheaval after the war, the ascendency of American entrepreneurialism and a time of economic health and stability. These ministries stepped into a void left by the institutional religious structures, which were not only suffering from theological and organizational conflict held over from the earlier decades of the twentieth century, but were also struggling to adapt to rapid cultural and social change. Such adaptability has always been a characteristic of apostolic structures and is particularly applicable in our own day. The very nature of these structures enables them to nimbly shift, adapt and adjust even amidst the most tumultuous social, political and technological changes.

In the 1980s, another crop of sodality structures emerged, sometimes referred to as the "baby-boomer, baby-buster ministries": Pioneers, Frontiers, CRM and others. At the beginning of the twenty-first century, there were over 1,700 entities accredited by ECFA (the Evangelical Council for Financial Accountability) in the United States—and that represents just the evangelical tradition.

LESSONS LEARNED

What observations can we draw from the Protestant experience?

1. Because they lack a centralized allegiance, it is more difficult for Protestants to maintain the necessary distinctions and separation between sodality and modality control. The essential distinctions become muddy because of inadequacies in Protestant missiological training and the popular misunderstanding of the sodality/modality distinction in the local churches, often perpetuated by well-meaning pastors and teachers.

2. Protestant apostolic structures can be divided into two general groups:

   a. Trans-denominational structures, which draw people from various theological traditions because their commitment to a common cause supersedes theological differences.

   b. Denominational structures, in which Protestant denominations create their own structures. For example, the International Mission Board of the Southern Baptist Convention—the largest denomination in the United States—has over five thousand people serving under its auspices. Not unlike the Catholic orders, the key to vibrancy and effectiveness for structures within denominations is maintaining healthy autonomy. Being co-opted by local church and/or denominational leadership may put these sodalities at risk. It is one of the inherent challenges for anyone pursuing an apostolic calling within a larger modality structure.

3. More than their Catholic counterparts, Protestant apostolic structures have the potential to morph into local church structures. This is a predictable sociological and organizational phenomenon that can result from a lack of centralized leadership, inadequate missiology and the propensity for those with the money and power to exercise control.

I was having lunch with a church leader from one of the old, reputable Protestant denominations in North America. He was responsible for their mission recruiting, training and sending efforts. His denomination was over 120 years old and had begun as a vibrant apostolic missionary movement. Over the years, it has morphed into a conservative, risk averse denominational structure that struggles to reassert an entrepreneurial spirit and vision.

In the course of the conversation I asked, "How long does it take from the time someone commits to serving with you as a missionary until you place them in an assignment around the world?"

"About seven years," he replied. My chin hit the soup.

This denomination frontloaded a stifling—if not overwhelming— amount of prerequisites into the training of their potential missionaries. There were educational requirements. There were years of internships and experience required. There were requirements for preparation in local churches. It was sad.

My next question was not very diplomatic. "So let me see if I understand this correctly. Your organization is doing a really good job, through your qualification criteria and vetting process, of weeding out anyone who has any sense of vision, calling or entrepreneurial spirit. What you are left with are the plodders who can endure your suffocating system. Right?" His head dropped. "Yes," was the reply.

While I admire the perseverance and tenacity of those who can work through such a process, the downside is that entrepreneurial personalities can be lost along the way.

4. Protestants are an interesting breed. On the whole, we are loath to learn from history. We often repeat our mistakes. That's understandable, considering our roots as a "protest" movement. That characteristic becomes even more exaggerated in North America, where we are influenced by the social dynamics of individualism and entrepreneurialism intrinsic to the American experience.

The result is that there are many streams and eddies in the Protestant portion of the Christian movement in North America, inside and outside of the traditional denominational structures: the missional church, the organic church, the simple church, the emerging church, a plethora of independent charismatic/Pentecostal churches, megachurches, house churches, new friars, neo-monastic groups, missional communities. . . . The distinctives and nuances go on and on and on.

But across the board, there is a lingering tendency—which goes all the way back to the Reformation—for Protestants to leave unclear the necessary distinction between sodality structures and modality structures, a distinction that is absolutely critical for the health of both. Further crippling our efforts is a lack of validation and appreciation for sodalities—specifically those that are apostolic in calling and focus—that bubbles up as an undercurrent in many Protestant streams. The Catholics and the Orthodox got it right when it comes to this distinction. We Protestants are still learning the lesson.

THE UNIQUE ROLE OF REVIVALS AND AWAKENINGS

In the Protestant tradition in North America, many have come to view the term *revival* in a negative light. It has unfortunately evolved to mean those periodic, often annual meetings held in some churches. These meetings are aggressively evangelistic, employing various forms of pressure, guilt and manipulation to coerce people onto the straight and narrow. Such meetings are only a faint echo of the revivalism of the eighteenth and nineteenth centuries and the great movements that periodically swept through North America.

Nevertheless, these services are an attempt to recreate an important spiritual and supernatural phenomenon that is a vital component to the health of the Christian movement as a whole and the submovements within it. Genuine revivals are those times when the Spirit of God manifests himself within the life of his people in great power, and there is an overwhelming encounter with the holiness and presence of God. The results spill out into the surrounding society in such a way that the society is awakened to spiritual reality, and every aspect of the social fabric is correspondingly transformed.

Probably the most eminent historian of genuine revivals and awakenings was J. Edwin Orr. Cambridge educated, he catalogued these remarkable moves of the Holy Spirit throughout history in over thirty books. Drawing on his meticulous research, I have come to some important conclusions.

1. Apostolic leaders and movements were invariably the *result* of revivals and awakenings, not the other way around. Apostolic leaders don't create the wave; rather, they surf the wave.

   Jonathan Edwards's ministry did not create the First Great Awakening. His ministry was a created by it. Evan Roberts was a leading figure of the Welsh Revival of 1904–1905, but he didn't cause it. Similarly, the winds of the worldwide revival and great awakening of 1858—sometimes called the Prayer Meeting Revival—blew life and momentum into the Salvation Army and energized its founders, William and Catherine Booth. The Salvation Army did not create the revival, but rather sailed in its wake.

2. Apostolic structures and apostolically gifted people have always been critical agents for capturing and pressing further the momentum of these spiritual outpourings. We see such people at crucial hinge-points as the spiritual fire spreads.

The Christian and Missionary Alliance, the YMCA, Young Life, the Navigators, Campus Crusade for Christ (Cru), the Billy Graham Association, the Student Volunteer Movement and countless other sodality structures are illustrations of this fact.

Sometimes these sovereign outpourings of the Holy Spirit are isolated. A good example is the Forest Home revival of 1949. I once heard J. Edwin Orr describe the details of this movement from his own experience, since he was one of the speakers at this extraordinary gathering. That revival had a profound effect on many who would become the Christian leaders of the post–World War II generation in North America: Billy Graham, Richard Halverson, Bill Bright, and others.

CRM experienced just such a unique outpouring in 1985 at Glen Eyrie, a retreat center in Colorado Springs. God manifested his presence in ways that were completely unexpected. The experience was characterized by a deep sense of holy awe, and with signs and wonders that were outside the paradigms to which any of us had been exposed. This sovereign move of God was not a part of our religious heritage. My wife had stayed in California to care for our two small children during the gathering. When I would call and try to convey to her what was happening, I had no words to express it. All I could do was sob on the phone because the presence of God was so profound.

The paradigms that shifted in us at that event—both personally and corporately—were significant. Within a year, we

were deploying our first personnel internationally and crossculturally. We became serious about starting and multiplying new
churches. Our frozen understandings of prayer were shattered
and we dove headlong into new—for us—ways of hearing from
God and plumbing the depths of a relationship with Jesus none
of us had dreamed possible.

This event in Colorado was a paradigm-bending experience
that was thoroughly biblical and completely consistent with
other times throughout history when God has stepped in and
spoken with great power to his people. The results and the ram-
ifications of that outpouring are still with us today, and the momentum it created has not waned.

3. A genuine outpouring of the Holy Spirit cannot be manufactured,
   manipulated or controlled. While prevailing prayer is always a
   factor and characteristic, it does not necessarily produce such supernatural phenomena. The Holy Spirit is like the wind, which
   "blows wherever it pleases. You hear its sound, but you cannot tell
   where it comes from or where it is going" (John 3:8).

   It is so human to want to capture a spiritual dynamic and put
   it in a box, to try to commoditize the extraordinary working of the
   triune God and reduce his holy prerogatives to formulas. But it
   simply does not work that way.

   What we can say with complete surety is that the creation and
   multiplication of apostolic structures and the calling of apostolic
   people who lead and work within them is a thoroughly supernatural process. It is a work of heaven. If apostolic structures are
   to be effective and long lasting, the Holy Spirit must be the wind
   in their sails. I have seen people try to generate such a dynamic
   on their own. They create a ministry or move to meet a need.
   While not necessarily illegitimate, such initiatives can fall completely flat without the anointing that only comes from on high.

   A need is not a call. Just because there is a need does not

necessarily mean that God has chosen me as the one to meet it. It is very common to start a ministry or begin an initiative and then watch it become like a sailing ship becalmed in still waters. Unless the Spirit of God moves in its sails, the ship is stuck. It does not matter how good the seamanship of the captain, or how seaworthy the ship. It must have the blessing and power of heaven.

THE CELTIC MOVEMENT

The history of the church overflows with accounts of God creating and using apostolic people to accomplish his kingdom purposes through apostolic structures beyond the local church. The evidence throughout the grand sweep of redemptive history is overwhelming.[9]

Such movements abound in all three of the major Christian traditions: the Roman Catholic tradition in the Western church, the Orthodox tradition in the East, and the Protestant tradition from 1517 forward (albeit mostly after the late eighteenth century). The pattern of apostolic people carrying out apostolic ministry is woven into the fabric of each. Wherever there have been men and women of abiding faith, obedient to Christ's commands to make disciples of all the nations, apostolic people, functions and structures proliferate. It is no surprise that the household of God is "built on the foundation of the apostles and prophets" (Ephesians 2:20).

Around AD 432, St. Patrick and a band of recruits arrived in Ireland. Supported by Pope Celestine I and the leadership of the British church, Patrick and his apostolic cohort launched what would become one of the premier examples of apostolic ministry in church history. Their work to evangelize Ireland and most of the rest of Europe spawned a movement that maintained apostolic fervency for many centuries through the multiplication of hundreds of monastic communities (sodalities) and, orbiting around them, thousands of local churches (modalities). As Steve Addison recounts:

For the next five hundred years, the youth of Ireland and their disciples fanned out across Europe, winning converts, making disciples and multiplying missionary outposts. . . . They revitalized European culture and possibly saved civilization following the fall of the Roman Empire.[10]

In multiple ways, the Celtic movement is a textbook case study of the dynamics of apostolic ministry and how it plays out in apostolic structures. The movement illustrates what apostolic people are all about and the interplay between the structures they create and the local church parishes around them. Patrick zealously maintained the distinctives between his apostolic bands and the local churches expressions that they multiplied. He intuitively understood the difference, and that was a significant part of the genius of his leadership.

CONTEMPORARY CELTS

These historical dynamics have been repeated over and over again throughout the fifteen hundred years since Patrick. These apostolic processes have been replayed in small ways beyond the gaze of historians. They have been duplicated in larger, more visible movements such as the Moravians, the Methodists, the Salvation Army, Youth With A Mission and many others who are striving to launch gospel movements in our own day.

We need these precedents to be newly contextualized in our own time and repeated more broadly and deeply than they ever have been in the past. We should beg and plead that history will repeat itself, with new generations of apostolic people being cut loose to soar. But I'm afraid if we hold our breath for existing local churches to catalyze such movements, we may quickly run out of air. As George Hunter observes, "No major denomination in the United States regards apostolic ministry to . . . pre-Christian outsiders as its priority or even as normal ministry."[11] However, there is much that we Westerners can learn from our brothers and sisters in other places around the world, where such gospel movements are the norm rather than the exception.

I was recently in a Middle Eastern country meeting with a dozen younger believers who were leading just such a movement. They had been at it for twenty-four months, and I asked for details. Over seventeen thousand people were in groups that were emerging into new churches, where an estimated twelve thousand (mostly from Muslim backgrounds) had become committed followers of Jesus. While these efforts were highly intentional, all this was being accomplished initially with no preachers, no teachers and no experts. It was a remarkable testimony of the power of the Bible and the manifest presence of the Holy Spirit. I can point to similar movements in other parts of the Middle East, as well as in South Africa, the horn of Africa, China and Southern Asia.

St. Patrick is alive and well. I've met many of his contemporary incarnations and their followers.

Does history repeat itself? Absolutely—and despite the demise of Christendom in the Western world, we are seeing the proliferation of such movements in our own day. This is God's doing. It is wonderful in his sight. And best of all, we get to partner with him in this grand adventure.

3

Mother Teresa Wasn't a "Para-Catholic"!

Why *parachurch* is a dirty word

The voluntary societies have been as revolutionary in their
effect as ever the monasteries were in their sphere.
The sodalities we now need may
prove equally disturbing.

Andrew F. Walls, "Missionary Societies and
Fortunate Subversion of the Church"

One should deliberately avoid speaking of
"church" and "para-church."

Arthur Glasser, *Announcing the Kingdom*

In my early days of ministry, I was gathering endorsements from
pastors that would be helpful in explaining our work to others.
One of our staff members had a relationship with the pastoral staff
of a prominent megachurch in California, so we were pleased that
an endorsement from the senior pastor was forthcoming. We
wanted some theological diversity in these endorsements, so we

especially appreciated the possibility of a letter from this pastor because of the tradition of the church that he represented. At least, that is what we thought until the letter arrived.

Dear Sam:

There is no way to get around the reality of the local church in the New Testament. It is obviously the institution established by God for our day.

It would also be God's desiring that strong local churches help establish other churches throughout the world. As a pastor in a church that is committed to this process, it is a thrill to see it happening.

There are numerous organizations who say their purpose is to be an "arm" of the church. However, in reality they never seem to make it happen. It is refreshing when a group like yours comes along. They not only state that their purpose is the local church, but it is also the very arena in which they labor.

I join the staff of CRM in praying that the need for their existence would become obsolete, because churches would obtain a healthy biblical perspective of ministry and would be reproductive in other flocks of believers. Until then, I know the Lord will continue to use the caring spirit in the men with CRM.

Yours in his service, [etc.]

When we received that letter, I was speechless. According to this pastor, we were illegitimate and unnecessary, and when local churches would finally rise to the occasion and be what he presumed they were supposed to be, sodalities would no longer be necessary. And until that time, the *men* would be surely blessed.

Needless to say, we never used this as an endorsement letter. However, I do use it regularly when orienting new people committing to vocational ministry as missionaries around the world. It helps illustrate a deficient and even aberrant ecclesiology in which the church in its local form is considered supreme and all else is "para"— or, even worse, illegitimate. A backhanded missile like this letter is sobering for new missionaries to see, since it represents some of the oppositional attitudes they may face. They need to know why such a perspective is theologically, historically and missiologically false.

EXORCISING "PARA"

A corrective form of discipline that was common in my home when I was a child was getting my mouth washed out with soap whenever I said something inappropriate or "talked back" to an adult in authority. Today such discipline would probably be considered a form of abuse, but for my generation growing up, it was an effective deterrent for control of the tongue.

When I am interacting with people new to ministry— especially those we're training to work in apostolic teams or communities—I often tell them there is one term that they should never use. If they do, they should wash their mouths out with soap. That's the term *parachurch*. It needs to be exorcised from our vocabulary. There is really no such thing. Either we're part of the church or we're not. And as we've seen from the Bible and history in chapters one and two, the church is not limited to its local form.

There are several reasons why the term *parachurch* has had such a detrimental effect on the Christian movement, particularly in the Protestant West:

1. *Para* can mean "not quite." So calling something "para" implies it's not the real or total deal. Think paramedic, paralegal or para-military. While they may serve and be alongside, someone who is labeled "para" never has total legitimacy in the eyes of the ones they serve.

2. The much-needed interdependence between the church local

(modality) and the church mobile (sodality) is stunted when one is considered whole and complete and the other is just "para." The relationship can too easily become one of control and dominance, not a genuine partnership.

3. The use of *parachurch* produces false expectations of what can and cannot be done in the local church context. If someone believes that the local expression of the church is all there really is or should be, then what God expects of the whole church will never be adequately met. That is because local churches and the denominational hierarchies in which they exist are, on their own, structurally incapable of fulfilling the full intentions of God for his people and his redemptive intentions for the world.

4. Talking in parachurch language can undermine and diminish the value of the apostolic calling, and the use of parachurch can make it harder to recruit those who should be ministering in apostolic structures. Why be a parachurch person when I could be in a pastoral or teaching position in a local church, and therefore be more fully "church"? Why be second-class?

Parachurch terminology reinforces an aberrant ecclesiology—what I call "the supremacy of the church local"—that is detrimental to the health and vibrancy of the Christian movement no matter where it is expressed.

WAS MOTHER TERESA A "PARA-CATHOLIC"?

This question itself shows how deficient the concept of parachurch is on face value. No one with a straight face would ever have called Mother Teresa a "para-Catholic." Nor would anyone label a Jesuit, a Dominican, a Franciscan or any of the other myriad of men and women committed to Catholic orders "para-Catholic." In fact, the opposite is the case.

Priests in the monastic tradition have been historically called *regular priests*. Priests caring for local parishes or diocese—meaning the modalic, ecclesiological hierarchy—have been called *secular priests*. The historical precedent in the Catholic tradition implies that secular priests were not as fully spiritual or cutting edge as those priests who had made second decision commitments to a religious order (see chapter six for a fuller discussion of "second decision" and "first decision"). Secular priests were not bound by a *regula* (a "rule"), which was a primary means of enforcing discipline and providing a platform for cohesion and mutual commitment to a common task.

Over the centuries this distinction has generated periodic conflict within the Catholic Church as these two complementary church expressions have jostled for position and status. One way in which the "secular" have sought to exert control over the "regular" (and to some extent they have been successful) has been in making ordination dependent on bishops, drawn from the secular clergy, who in turn populate the hierarchy. But overall, the Catholics have carved out an effective balance between the two categories, which has been a major factor in Catholic spiritual and organizational vitality. As Ralph Winter comments:

> The harmony between the modality and the sodality achieved by the Roman Church is perhaps the most significant characteristic of this phase [the Medieval period] of the world Christian movement and continues to be Rome's greatest organizational advantage to this day.[1]

THE SUPREMACY OF THE CHURCH LOCAL

The Protestant Reformation's missiological failure of rejecting apostolic, missionary structures had profound repercussions that still reverberate today. One of the lingering results is the concept of "the supremacy of the church local" that unfortunately remains among some pastors and denominational leaders within Protestantism.

"The supremacy of the church local" is the view that the church in its local form is the only legitimate expression of the body of Christ. In this view, the local congregation or diocese or parish is the only true expression of what "church" truly is. The concept of parachurch flows directly out of this truncated, inadequate concept of the church. There are several reasons why the supremacy of the church local continues to have traction.

Many of those who lead local churches and denominational structures have never heard or learned anything different. It's an educational blind spot. Countless times, I've heard pastors and other leaders say, "I've never heard any of this before," regarding the legitimacy of apostolic structures and anything outside of their local purviews. It even spills over into the general church culture and is reinforced by the traditional religious establishment. As George Barna notes:

> There is a pervasive mind-set among many journalists, scholars, and religious leaders that all legitimate spiritual activity must flow through a local church. Even large parachurch ministries that communicate with tens of millions of people, raise hundreds of millions of dollars, and impact lives all over the world are cast as second fiddle to the local church. It is almost as if their ministry efforts are deemed subpar simply because they did not originate from a congregational context.[2]

Charles Mellis accurately states :

> The leadership of nurture structures (congregations and linkage structures) on whom we largely depend for our Christian education has always tended to a mono-structural view of the church. In fact, our theologians tend to define the church in terms of this nurture structure.[3]

Unfortunately, this truncated view of the church as valid only in its local form has prevailed, as Mellis notes, in Western theological education *except* in the field of missiology. Missionaries and other apostolically gifted individuals have been traditionally required to endure a classic theological curriculum, including Greek, Hebrew and other topics that are more relevant for life in the academy or, secondarily, to local congregations. To get duly certified for ministry, missionaries have had to jump through the hoops of an educational system too often biased toward the scholarly or pastoral. Thankfully, in forward-looking educational institutions, that has begun to change.

Conversely, those headed into pastoral ministry or hierarchal "linkage structures" (that is, denominations) rarely have to immerse themselves in missiological studies. As I once heard a missionary lament, "I have to learn all their stuff, which is largely irrelevant and useless where I'm going, but they never have to study any of our stuff. They don't have a clue what apostolic ministry—particularly in international and crosscultural settings—is all about."

It is an exceptional pastor who is exposed to the theology of mission, missional ecclesiology or the history of movements. While they may have studied church history from the perspective of doctrine, heresies and apologetics, they seldom examine the fundamental structural dynamics that are essential for an understanding of the health and expansion of the greater Christian movement. Few ever wrestle with Kenneth Scott Latourette's *A History of Christianity* or any of the seminal missiology of the likes of Lesslie Newbigin, Donald McGavran, Charles Van Engen, Alan Hirsch or David Bosch. As Alan Hirsch once told me, "Those in charge of both the educational institutions that provide the credentialing for those headed into ministry vocations as well as the local church expressions that harbor most of the resources are pastors and teachers."[4] In *The Permanent Revolution*, Hirsch elaborates:

> The current training system was started and is still operated

by the teacher and shepherd of the APEST [apostles, prophets, evangelists, shepherds and teachers, from Ephesians 4] typology. One has to wonder what a system designed by and for a fully-fledged APEST ministry would look like. What would change? What would be the likely outcomes?[5]

I find this deficiency also in some of the conversations among those longing to recapture a sense of missionality in the local church and its denominational structures in the West. I hear Western pastors and others debating missional issues and concerns that are frankly old hat in the global missions community.

I was participating in a small gathering that included some of the more prominent pastors in the North American Protestant church. Also in the room were those representing an array of creative, innovative local church expressions on the national scene—cell churches, "organic" churches, the missional church and new networks and movements, all representing a broad background of traditions: Anglicans, Southern Baptists, Presbyterians and Pentecostals, along with numerous independent bodies. We were discussing together how to recover the function of apostolic ministry in the present-day Christian movement in North America.

Interestingly, I was the only one representing a mission organization, and one of the few coming at the discussion from a practical stance other than the leadership of a local church, denomination or "network" structure. After the first day of the conference I began to sense what a unique posture that was. The best way I can describe it is that it was like being a Jesuit in a room full of bishops all longing to restore Jesuit-like functions to their local parishes and diocese structures. The problem was that there were almost no other Jesuits in the room. And in the conversation there was very little understanding of the essential structures necessary to see their vision accomplished. As I listened, I observed several reasons for this lack.

First, almost all of these leaders were operating from the posture of local church ministry. As such, they were deeply committed to the local church and deeply desirous of biblical missionality being expressed to its fullest in the local church context. They didn't want to give up on their local churches becoming more missional.

Second, I sensed that most had bought into the deficient ecclesiology of the supremacy of the church local. As one megachurch pastor commented to me, "I've always taught my people that missionary entities like yours only exist because the local church isn't doing what it's supposed to do. Now you're telling me that's not true?"

By no fault of their own, most had been trained in our Western seminaries and theological colleges where pastors, teachers and academics predominate and where ecclesiology is rarely influenced by missiology—if it is at all. Most of the people in the room were victims of our deficient theological system.

Here was a room of brilliant men and women wrestling with what many of them perceived to be "new" missional insights and with how to apply them to churches in North America. But there was very little that was new about their conclusions. These were issues that have been front-and-center in missiological discussions within sodality circles for many decades, but have only recently begun to be applied in the rapidly shifting church culture of North America and Western Europe.

As the West has increasingly become a legitimate mission field, it has been encouraging to see leaders such as these begin to think and act missiologically. On the other hand, it is disappointing that their conversations rarely include the apostolic people or the apostolic agencies that have been dealing with substantive missiological issues since the beginning of the modern missionary movement in 1792. That's over two hundred years of important lessons. Fortunately, some of these contemporary leaders gravitate toward this understanding intuitively, particularly when they themselves create apostolic structures to accomplish what they cannot do within their modalities.

This lack of understanding is spread across a broad spectrum, from the traditional/historic churches of modernity, including contemporary megachurches (which are particularly susceptible because of their perceptions of self-sufficiency), to the missional and emerging church expressions as they grapple to relate to present-day culture.

Yet when leaders—pastoral, lay and those leading apostolic structures—all get it, the resulting synergy that occurs from such a biblical, Spirit-directed interdependence is a tremendous thing to experience. And when it genuinely happens, the probability that the name of Jesus will be renowned among the nations in an Ephesians 3:20 kind of way—"immeasurably more than all we ask or imagine"—becomes more of a genuine reality.

Leaders, particularly pastoral leaders, genuinely believe the supremacy of the church local. Clinging to the supremacy of the church local can be an honest attempt to jealously—in a good sense—keep the pressure on the local church to live and operate missionally. I've been in discussions with pastoral leadership who, despite all the evidence, refuse to embrace the legitimacy of sodalities, particularly those structures in which people with strong apostolic, missionary gifting can flourish. I've had well-meaning pastors admit that they simply can't acknowledge this reality because they don't want to give up on their expectation that apostolic outcomes can be fully exercised within and through their own congregations. Embracing the two-structure, two-footed paradigm would somehow mean abandoning the ideal of what they believe local churches could and should be. I believe the motivation of these pastors is noble, but their fear is unfounded.

In helping these leaders toward a more complete ecclesiology, I encourage them to do their best to imbed apostolic *values* and *vision* within their congregations. But I also ask them to not selfishly hang onto apostolic people who may find greater fulfillment in structures beyond the local church.

Every local church expression should strongly exhort its members or congregants to live missionally, particularly in the context of near-neighbor relationships—which include family, work and community. But living missionally in our near-neighbor context is quite different from deployment as a second decision person who may cross cultural, social, linguistic and, when necessary, geographic barriers for the sake of the gospel. Those people committed together with others to second decision vocations need structures specifically designed for them if they are to be successful. Local churches should send or attach such people to existing structures, or create the structures and give them the autonomy and support necessary to flourish.

There is a fear of embracing the full meaning of Ephesians 4. In chapter five we'll examine Ephesians 4 and the idea of apostolic calling. One of the reasons contributing to the concept of the supremacy of the local church local is that a biblical understanding of apostolic gifting or apostolic ministry is usually sorely lacking at the local church level. Most local church and denominational settings provide little understanding and appreciation of the APEST taxonomy [Apostles, Prophets, Evangelists, Shepherds and Teachers] in Ephesians 4.

One reason it has been ignored is that most local churches are led by pastors and teachers. Their leadership is to be expected, since those structures are primarily for the care and nurture of first decision people. That's the context in which pastoral leaders thrive. Unfortunately, pastoral leaders rarely know what to do with those who begin to demonstrate and live out apostolic calling. When someone with apostolic giftedness emerges, local churches have a remarkable tendency to squash them, marginalize them or label them as rebels. As Mellis observes:

> The nurture structures down through history have been loath to provide such channels, and slow to bless those that have emerged. In fact, they have often clawed at the heels of those members who have reached out for deeper forms of commitment.[6]

People with apostolic gifts can cause a good deal of angst for pastoral leaders. Often these apostolic troublemakers and the poor pastors who try to cope with them don't understand where the tension is coming from, and the resulting conflicts are too often characterized as spiritual in nature. It's the same dynamic clearly evident in Acts 9, as the Jerusalem church struggled to cope with Paul.

In my early years of ministry I didn't understand this dynamic, and I often found myself in difficult situations. I was personally bruised, and I needlessly bruised others. As I moved into positions of leadership, I had to learn how to steward apostolic rabble-rousers (some of whom were very much like me). They needed to be coached with a long tether and a high degree of autonomy. Their entrepreneurial spirits—sometimes fragile—had to be encouraged and given plenty of room to roam. I also saw how their energy and vision could invigorate a local congregation. When these dynamics were successful, it was usually due in no small part to a patient, secure pastor in the mix.

However, a pastor ultimately may need to release the person, particularly if their vision and gifts cannot be contained in one local setting. Give them away! Attach them to apostolic structures where they can attain their full God-given potential. Let them soar.

ALIGNING MISSIONAL EXPECTATIONS

Some pastors and denominational leaders may be reluctant to embrace apostolic gifts or structures because of a misunderstanding about what local churches are best at, and particularly how local church expressions multiply.

We desperately need more and healthier local churches. Hundreds of millions of those who follow Jesus find their spiritual homes in these local bodies. These churches are where the overwhelming majority of followers of Jesus will grow, be nurtured and flourish as his disciples. That is because local settings are the essential, cross-generational structure that conserves the fruit of the Christian movement.

But the local church will never be the primary structure that pioneers new ground, particularly when barriers must be crossed for the sake of the good news of Jesus. Rarely are modalities on the cutting edge of the new. They are, by their very nature, risk averse and designed to conserve.

Local churches preserve what already exists, provide a place where all can belong, and when healthy press for deeper commitment and vibrant spirituality. Such local parishes are particularly effective in their own immediate cultural milieu and can exercise an enormous transformational kingdom impact if they are committed to living out a holistic gospel in word, deed and power among near-neighbors. As Wagner says,

> The modality is essentially a people-oriented structure, designed to serve the people who are part of it. Peace and harmony are high values. *Being* is seen as superior to *doing*. Process is often more important than goal. Discipleship is usually not strictly applied, especially when it might clash with contentment.[7]

Local church expressions have never been blessed by God to do in scope what the apostolic and missionary structures are able to do. It's unfair to expect local churches to have the same sense of discipline and focus as the apostolic forms of the church.

For example, I know of no missiologist who would disagree with the fact that the multiplication of the local church is an essential outcome of Christ's Great Commission in Matthew 28. The multiplication of new church expressions is one of the primary results when that commission has been carried out in practice over the two thousand years since Pentecost. It is the story of the book of Acts, as the church went from simply adding people to its number to multiplying (Acts 6:1-7).

However, I cringe when I hear well-meaning pastors or other "experts" on church planting talk about "local churches planting local churches" as if it were the only way such multiplication takes place. That's simply not the way it has happened throughout the centuries, and it's a false expectation to place on local congregations, particularly as an expectation for missionality that is more than near-neighbor.

MOST LOCAL CHURCHES ARE EUNUCHS

So what should we expect from the church in its local form? Local churches should definitely be expected to inculcate missionality and live it out, to be reproductive individually and corporately in their immediate, near-neighbor context and to be supportive of crosscultural missionality that extends to the nations. We should expect local church expressions to add people to their number through conversion *and* to multiply within their own cultural milieu—what missiologists would call "near-neighbor" evangelism, or E-0 and, in some contexts, E-1.

These terms come from a scale—actually a continuum—that missiologists use to describe cultural distance in the evangelistic task.[8] E-0 is ministry within one's own cultural context. E-1 is ministry with some minor cultural distance, and E-2 and E-3 are increasing levels of cultural distance and dissonance.

Even when local churches attempt E-0 efforts, their ministry can be more effective when done in tandem with apostolic people working in apostolic structures. But the more barriers are present—E-1 through E-3—the more needful and appropriate it is for unique apostolic structures to be created to shoulder the primary ministry responsibility.

Sadly, even with this expectation of near-neighbor missionality, most local churches are eunuchs—they don't reproduce or plant other churches. Effective multiplication among near neighbors is rarely lived out. Missionality beyond near-neighbors happens even less. Despite the wishful thinking and cajoling of those desperately wanting to see a new birth of apostolic vision and passion throughout local church life, they are pumping water uphill if they expect the church in its local form to take on all the functions of an apostolic, missionary sodality.

The church in its local form is not structured for life that way. Its people are sociologically incapable of that type of behavior no matter how much they are exhorted, trained or encouraged, primarily because they are first decision people. However, when apostolically gifted people in a local church are given the permission and the structural means to move toward second decision living— where they commit vocationally to a sodality—then an apostolic, missionary expression can be born.

I want to be clear. Local churches have a vital and important missional role to play in sustaining movements of the gospel. "Ecclesia ought always to be movemental to some degree, or it ceases to be the church that Jesus intended it to be."[9] But too often, particularly in the West, the inadequate church planting models which we have uncritically adopted stifle missional momentum, and rarely result in movements. We're not even experiencing the near-neighbor multiplication that can be reasonably expected from all local congregations.

Of the 400,000 churches in the United States, only a few can be considered reproductive and fruitful. For instance, Neil Cole, reflecting on research done by the Southern Baptist research and resource center, Lifeway, notes that only four percent of Southern Baptist churches in the United States will plant a daughter church. Extrapolated across the denominations, that means that 96 percent of the conventional churches in the United States will never give birth.[10]

Consider a military analogy. No one would take the doctors, cooks and logistics personnel in the military and make them all serve on Special Forces missions. Different people are needed for different roles. This principle holds true for those in local congregations. It is unreasonable to expect first decision people to act like second decision people—a distinction that we will develop in the coming chapters. We can't expect every soldier to be a Navy SEAL. While we would want Mother Teresa's values to be inculcated into every follower of Jesus, how unreasonable would it be to expect every committed follower of Jesus to adopt her lifestyle and live out her monastic, missionary calling?

It's like asking everyone to have two left feet. George Lings writes,

> In my city of Sheffield, as a citizen I am a modal member of a diverse society of all ages, along with ½ million others. We are the most common and numerous. But Sheffield has sodalities; they include the Fire service and the Police Force. Its members are also citizens, but they have a second calling and resultant equipping to a particular role. They form special bonds of comradeship in those sodal groups. I cannot, however much it might be fun, roll up to the fire station tomorrow and ask to go out to the next call. It doesn't work like that.[11]

Hirsch and Catchim explain it this way:

> How we structure organization has a direct impact on outcomes—for good or for ill—and leadership must be aware of

the implications and face the consequences. . . . It is no good trying to build a revived apostolic ministry and structure around forms and organizations that are built to deliver something fundamentally different.[12]

The implications of this understanding are profound. Apostolic, missionary structures do things local church expressions cannot do. When unrealistic expectations are placed upon local churches, they cannot help but fail to meet those expectations.

For example, I get weary of hearing the oft-repeated mantra that "the local church is the hope of the world." It's simply not true. The church in its local form is not all that there is. Such a false expectation justifies George Barna's sobering observation: "If we place all our hope in the local church, it is a misplaced hope. Many well-intentioned pastors promote this perspective by proclaiming, 'The local church is the hope of the world'. . . . If the local church is the hope of the world, then the world has no hope."[13] Barna is right. As the Bible and history so clearly show us, if we depend solely on the church in its local form, there is no hope—and there never has been.

THE RELEVANCE OF BLACK VESTMENTS

I was taking a tour of the Church of Scotland's beautiful Glasgow Cathedral, which is technically the High Kirk of Glasgow. It is estimated that over 50,000 university students live within walking distance of this extraordinary building. The congregation of the church itself is down to a remnant of less than two hundred people. So I purposely asked the docent leading the tour, "If this building still houses an active congregation, what is being done to reach these 50,000 students with the good news of Jesus?" Her response was stunning.

"The people we have who are active in this church are mostly old.

And as you may well know," she said, "young people these days are not
that interested in religion. But we're trying and we're making adjustments. For example, the Church of Scotland has historically used black
or dark vestments for our clergy. But recently, to be more relevant,
we've added color!" I was so stunned I could barely contain myself.

So who is going to reach those 50,000 students who are far from
God? The High Kirk of Glasgow isn't, despite its use of colored vestments. If there are going to be any inroads among the student population, it will probably require apostolic efforts—and the more the
better. And as those apostolic structures and missionaries are effective, their efforts will result in the creation of countless new local
church expressions among students, expressions that probably will
not look anything like the High Kirk of Glasgow.

Those new local church expressions will be essential for conserving the fruit of the apostolic, missionary efforts among this
specific segment of the population. If a movement is to occur, it will
require dynamic cooperation between these missionary efforts and
the resulting local church expressions. Because the present generation's disillusionment with the status quo, most of the new local
church expressions that are either born or renewed will probably
be new wineskins. They will embody vibrant Christian orthodoxy,
but in forms that bear little resemblance to the traditional, institutional expressions of the church that are dying around them. Ex-
pecting the High Kirk of Glasgow to be the agent of change after
eight hundred years is beyond hope apart from the dramatic inter-
vention of the Spirit of God.

Re:Hope is a case study of just such missional activity. Re:Hope
is a new local church expression started in Glasgow during the last
decade through the efforts of a CRM missionary team—an apostolic structure. Re:Hope has now evolved into one of the largest,
most dynamic and thriving ministries in the city. With an emphasis
of using and reading the Bible interpersonally, coupled with em-

bracing the manifest presence and power of the Holy Spirit, Re:Hope has evolved into a contagious missional body engaging a generation that is thirsty and desperate for spiritual reality in a post-Christian culture. Re:Hope is a good example of what can happen when apostolic structures and local church structures work in healthy interdependence.[14]

THE NEED FOR MORE

The point is that more apostolic, missionary structures brimming with apostolic people are always needed. Lots of them! We can never have enough ministries like Youth With A Mission, Young Life, Sisters of Mercy, Cru, the Salvation Army, the International Mission Board, InterVarsity, Frontiers, Pioneers, the Franciscans, Word Made Flesh, International Justice Mission, The Navigators, and on and on. The proliferation and multiplication of such structures has always been a sign of health in the Christian movement.

The numbers bear this out. Young Life, for example, claims that they relationally reach and impact 1.7 million kids each year. The Jesus Film—part of Cru—estimates 3.8 million people decide to follow Jesus every year as a result of viewing the film. InterVarsity field staff minister to 40,299 core students and faculty on 616 campuses in North America and as a part of IFES, which has a ministry presence in 154 countries. Youth With A Mission has over 16,000 long-term workers ministering out of 1,000 bases in over 180 countries. While these are just a few of the major examples, there are thousands upon thousands of such apostolic expressions of the church. And wherever we see movements of the gospel take off, these expressions are *always* in the mix.

IN THE ZONE IN THE MIDDLE EAST

I met him while traveling and working in the Middle East. Let's call him Deioces—the name of a famous mythical king of the Medes.

Deioces's father had been killed in Iran because he was a follower of Jesus, and Deioces had fled with his family to northern Iraq. Although he was part of a small, traditional church with a focus on the Medes, Deioces was obviously chafing at the limitations of this local fellowship. Even though he was only in his early twenties, he oozed apostolic giftedness and vision, but he lacked the vehicle for it to be adequately expressed.

Today, with our help and partnership, Deioces is at the nexus of a burgeoning movement of the gospel, particularly among Syrian and Iraqi refugees fleeing the Syrian civil war. Thousands have found new life in Jesus and have become committed disciples through this movement. And Deioces has not had an upfront, visible role. Initially there was no preaching or teaching or large gatherings of people. Deioces has learned and relentlessly applied simple movement dynamics, and the results have been stunning.

He's realized that planting churches never guarantees that a movement will result, but that generating healthy movements will always result in new church expressions. He's figured out how to identify "persons of peace" in that context—consistent with Jesus' instructions in Matthew 10, Mark 6 and Luke 9 and 10—and how such persons can be keys to unlocking whole people groups to become disciples of Jesus. And he's adopted a simple discovery process whereby people far from God can explore the Bible together while being open to the supernatural presence and work of God's Spirit.

Foundational to Deioces's effectiveness is the surety of his apostolic calling and the platform for it to be lived out. He's not "para" to anything. He's in the zone of what God has made him to be, and the results are awesome.

So *parachurch* really is a dirty word. The health and vibrancy of the Christian movement, wherever it is found, depends on sodalities, and particularly those sodalities where apostolic people are allowed to be all that God designed them to be—fully church and fully released to be agents of the kingdom, in places where local church expressions aren't able to pioneer.

4

So What Is "Apostolic"?

The oft-neglected essential to
authentic missionality

Ἀπόστολος: *One sent as a messenger or agent,
the bearer of a commission, messenger; an apostle.*

The Analytical Greek Lexicon

*The apostle is the quintessentially missional form of ministry
and leadership. The apostolic role provides the key that
unlocks the power of New Testament ecclesiology
insofar as its ministry is concerned.*

Alan Hirsch & Tim Catchim, *The Permanent Revolution*

*There is little point in breeding tigers if you intend
to keep them chained up in dog kennels.*

George Lings, "Why Modality and Sodality Thinking
Is Vital to Understand Future Church"

I met Jeff sitting in a course at a seminary. He was 29, married with two kids, finishing his degree and holding down a role on a pastoral staff in south-central Los Angeles—and he was frustrated beyond description.

He was a strong, godly leader with clear apostolic gifting. He oozed with potential. But serving in a pastoral role had been a serious mismatch between who he was and the expectations of a local church. I wasn't sure which would happen first—his local church killing him or him killing it!

I meet people like Jeff on a regular basis: men and women with apostolic fervor and passion desperately thrashing around to find their niche in ministry. And all too many have been led to believe that the only path they can travel to fulfill God's calling on their lives is to climb the pastoral ladder in a local church setting. How tragic.

The historical, biblical, sociological and missiological fact is that strong apostolic gifting—particularly for those called to live as second decision people—is best lived out in an apostolic structure (a type of sodality) in order for such gifting to be adequately fulfilled.

Until such young leaders, both men and women, find their niche in apostolic structures where they can move beyond maintenance to missionality and be cut loose to see their vision soar, their lives will be models of frustration with a numbing lack of meaning.

Eddie Gibbs, professor emeritus at Fuller Seminary, notes that 50 percent of those who graduate from North American seminaries and who eventually end up in pastoral ministry drop out within ten years. My guess is that an uncomfortable percentage of that number is made up of men and women just like Jeff.

So there is hope for Jeff and others like him. You're not crazy! You're not a rebel. There is nothing wrong with you. Your ambition, drive and desire to accomplish much with Jesus and for his kingdom are not unholy. May God lead you to the right apostolic, missionary structure where you can make your ultimate contribution to the kingdom and live the way God has uniquely made you to be.

TO CAMBODIA, ROMANIA AND BEYOND

Diane was another person like this. After university, she worked in the business world as an accountant for a national business systems firm, all the while restless and worried that she was not fulfilling God's unique calling on her life. We met Diane in the midst of that struggle when she was on a short-term trip to Hungary, and over time we helped her sort it out. She joined InnerCHANGE[1]—a Christian order among the poor—and ultimately left corporate life to be part of a team in Cambodia that rescued girls from the sex trade. She went on to provide visionary leadership to a comprehensive AIDS prevention and treatment program in the Cambodian countryside called Sunrise, which continues to be a model for the whole nation. She led a pioneering team ministering among the poor and marginalized in Romania for several years, and most recently has assumed administrative leadership for 125 similar missionaries serving among the poor worldwide. Along the way she has immersed herself in becoming language proficient in each of these settings. Because she has apostolic gifting, Diane is uniquely suited for ministry of such scope and diversity, and is a remarkable example of the way God can use such a person if they are given the appropriate structures in which to flourish.

APOSTOLIC—THE DIFFERENT VIEWS

When I help prepare people to minister around the world with CRM, I often do presentations on how to identify, challenge and provide a place for those whose calling would be well fulfilled in our ministry. It's an initiation into "our tribe." At the top of the list of qualities I look for is "apostolic gifting." But what is apostolic gifting and how is it identified?

Much has been written about this. Some authors use the term *missionary gifting* interchangeably with *apostolic gifting*. Others struggle to find a biblical basis for the missionary gift, since it is only implied in Scripture and is not overtly mentioned in the three lists of spiritual gifts in the New Testament. Others draw a clear distinction between *missionary* and *apostolic* and consider them both highly relevant (and overlooked) in the contemporary church. Still others dismiss the term *apostolic* altogether as irrelevant in this dispensation. There are lots of opinions.

I like the way Mike Breen describes apostolic ministry in his book *The Apostle's Notebook* and the paradigm he presents.[2] Basing his analysis on the life of Jesus, Breen says that apostolic ministry has four distinct tasks inherent in it:

1. Pioneering

2. Planting

3. Bridging

4. Building

Breen takes the bulk of his book to unpack these four tasks and the way they work at the ground level for people who have an apostolic calling. He makes a strong argument in his exegesis of Ephesians 4 that everyone in the Church functions either as an apostle, prophet, evangelist, pastor or teacher. He bases this conclusion on the textual evidence as well as his extensive first-hand experience.

Another thorough treatment of apostolic ministry and gifting in contemporary ministry is Alan Hirsch and Tim Catchim's excellent volume, *The Permanent Revolution*.[3] They comprehensively lay out the theological case for apostolic calling and ministry. It is a superb and exhaustive text and a thoughtful apologetic for the legitimacy and pursuit of apostolic ministry in the present-day church. Their exegesis of Ephesians 4 and the nature of the APEST taxonomy

(Apostles, Prophets, Evangelists, Shepherds and Teachers) is masterful. While their chapter "Apostolic Architecture: The Anatomy of Missional Organization" is one of the better treatments of the topic that I know of, my hope is that what I am writing in this book can build on that foundation and be an expanded argument for the necessity of such structures where apostolic gifting and calling can be most fully lived out.

Alan and Tim make the sobering claim that

> insofar that it depends on human agency, the church's capacity to embody and extend the mission and purposes of Jesus in the world depends largely on a full-intention to provide robust theoretical foundations with which to relegitimize and restructure the ministry of the church as fivefold and to reembrace the revitalizing, intrinsically missional role of the apostolic person.[4]

I think there are few better summaries as to the nature of apostolic gifting than their summary:

> In the power of the Holy Spirit, apostles are given to the ecclesia to provide the catalytic, adaptive, movemental, translocal, pioneering, entrepreneurial, architectural, and custodial ministry needed to spark, mobilize, and sustain apostolic movements.[5]

I've seen a fear among many to embrace apostolic gifting—and the apostolic function referred to in Ephesians 4—because of perceived abuses that occur at what I call the "macro" level of apostolic engagement. That is when someone—perhaps a leader in a movement—assumes, sometimes presumptuously, that they are the "apostle" to a city or a region. They may exercise what some call "vertical" or "horizontal" apostolic oversight[6] and may exercise authority over a large constituency of the body of Christ, like a kind of superpastor. There are numerous movements, particularly within charismatic and Pentecostal wings of the

Christian movement, that have embraced this phenomenon in recent years, described as the "New Apostolic Reformation." However, that is not an approach that I'm comfortable with, and that is not how I am using the term in this book.

I appreciate the distinction that Hirsch and Catchim make between big "A" Apostles (the original twelve) and little "a" apostles (all those, past and present, who have exhibited apostolic giftedness and functions). I believe the biblical evidence is abundantly clear that the term "apostle" was never relegated to mean just the original twelve.[7] Hirsch and Catchim further define what apostles do:

> Apostles, then and now, have an irreplaceable purpose in maintaining ongoing missional capacities, generating new forms of ecclesia, and working for the continual renewing of the church, among many other vital functions. As central and important as Scripture is, it was never meant to replace the dynamic missional function of the apostles in Jesus' church.[8]

I prefer not to be drawn into the argument about whether or not apostolic gifting exists in the present day, because I believe it is a waste of time. It is my conviction that a cessationist view is indefensible exegetically—and certainly experientially as well—in light of the overwhelming historical evidence. There are over eighty references in the New Testament to apostles, which clearly refer to more than the original twelve. The existence and legitimacy of the apostolic gift is clearly a given in Scripture. For my purposes, other questions are more important: What is it? What do we do with it? And what are the implications for missional structures?

DEFINING APOSTOLIC

When I refer to the apostolic gift, the definition I am using at its most basic is simply "a sent one." It is a spiritual gift no different than any of the others available to those who follow Jesus and is distributed at the Spirit's pleasure, whether vested or occasional. In other words, I believe it is most useful to consider the gift and its function at a micro level (the little "a" apostolic). I believe that is more in line with the function found in the fivefold description in Ephesians 4. Thus the way I prefer to use the term includes the following.

- Apostolic people are cut out to cross barriers—cultural, linguistic, socio-economic and geographic—for the sake of the spread of Jesus' gospel (Pauline), or focus on the vibrancy and vigor of existing expressions of the church for the sake of greater missionality (Petrine).

- Practically speaking, those with an apostolic gift are spiritual entrepreneurs. They display a keen sense of adventure, they innovate and they embrace the new—sometimes just because it's new. They desire to create, build and expand the frontiers of the Christian movement. They don't conserve. They don't maintain. They exhibit a sense of rebelliousness which, unless sanctified, can make life difficult for those around them. They often exhibit a holy discontent—a kind of a ministry ADHD.

- Many times, people with an apostolic gift also have a missionary ability (or gift), meaning the calling and skills to exercise an apostolic function in crosscultural venues.

- Apostolic people often have the capacity to uniquely minister to pastors and other church leaders. They have the maturity, spiritual authority, vision and ability to influence other leaders.

- Apostolic people are often able to minister in a context broader than a single local church. They have a larger perspective and the scope of their vision is greater than one local congregation.

- They value results over conformity, chaos over control and vision over stability. They push the limits. They can cause trouble and angst for the establishment. As George Hunter observes in his classic little book, *The Celtic Way of Evangelism*, "In most American denominations . . . the people who control the denomination are the same people who are less apostolic in their emphasis. . . . Their special obsession is to control the growing wing of the church and 'correct' it. . . . As one wag so aptly observed, 'It is always easier to preside over a graveyard than it is over a kindergarten.' Apostolic people prefer the mess over the alternative."[9]

• While fundraising and living on money given by others can be a stretch for anyone, those with apostolic gifting are not overly daunted by this challenge. Often they embrace it. They see it as a mountain to climb and an obstacle to overcome for the sake of a greater kingdom vision.

• People with an apostolic gift are most likely to be fulfilled in apostolic sodalities, that is, structures specifically suited for the fullest expression of their gifts. If they are second decision people, this is where most of them belong.

IT'S NEVER VERY NEAT

It's time for a few caveats. First, I am biased. There is definitely some gift projection going on in the way I define and use the term apostolic.

Second, I believe that all spiritual gifts operate on a continuum and in combinations, or as J. Robert Clinton would say, "in clusters."[10] The characteristics I've listed above are demonstrated to various degrees and various levels, particularly when grouped with other gifts. There are shades and variations to this theme.

Third, I don't believe anyone should overreact as they scrutinize their own life in light of these qualities. Often in marriages, for example, one spouse with an apostolic gift may lean this way more than the other. If the couple is serving in an essentially apostolic ministry, it may mean some dissonance and adjustment. At the very least, it will mean understanding, appreciating and embracing such a gift and its implications.

And finally, I believe that for an apostolic structure to be healthy, the majority of those ministering in it permanently must, to one degree or another, exhibit an apostolic gift in their "cluster" of gifts. There is certainly room—and need—for those with other gifts who will complement this primary thrust. Diversity is a good thing and some balance is useful. But to maintain its integrity and calling, an apostolic structure must always be characterized by an apostolic DNA, which is represented by the gifts of those who serve within the structure. It's the very nature of such ministry. It's in the values, and in the essence of God's collective calling for them as an entity.

Therefore, it can be risky for an apostolic structure to place someone with strong pastoral or teaching gifts in charge. Having such a person in leadership can inhibit the apostolic momentum. This issue may have fundamentally been at the root of the conflict between Paul and Barnabas in Acts 15:39. Paul had a strong apostolic gift, and he came into conflict with Barnabas, the "son of encouragement," who was relational, gracious and kind—characteristics not usually attributed to the hard-driving Paul. Barnabas had strong pastoral gifting, which is normally unsuitable for ongoing leadership in an apostolic structure. As Wagner states:

> Barnabas clearly fits the profile of what some missiologists today would call a "modality leader," as opposed to Paul who would have been seen as a "sodality leader." I suppose that about 80 percent of ordained clergy are like Barnabas and essentially people-oriented, and only about 20 percent might be task-oriented sodality types like Paul. . . . Subsequent centuries of church history have revealed that in an active, dynamic mission organization there is ordinarily room for only one leader or apostle. There were not two Hudson Taylors in the China

> Inland Mission, or two Dawson Trotmans in the Navigators, or
> two Cameron Townsends in Wycliffe Bible Translators.[11]

Later, Wagner goes on:

> Paul's consecrated pragmatism surfaces when he seems to
> care less about hurting the feelings of Mark and Barnabas
> than he does about being certain in his own mind that his
> mission team is as highly competent and qualified as possible
> to accomplish the formidable task just ahead of them.[12]

Conversely, it is unusual for someone with strong apostolic gifting
to survive the demands of the typical local church. Occasionally such
a person may become the pastor, and if given enough freedom and
room to lead, the ministry of that local church can thrive. If that apostolic leader can endure the rocky ride, such churches may grow into
megachurches. I can't name or think of a single person who has led a
local church into megachurch status who did not have some measure
of apostolic gifting. And usually they have little or no pastoral gifting
either. They may carry the title "pastor," but that's a misnomer. Their
success is often dependent on their ability to recruit others around
them (that is, people with pastoral gifting) who can care for the people
and free an apostolically gifted leader to do the pioneering.

PEOPLE WHO DON'T FIT

When I orient our new personnel at CRM, I often cite two stanzas
from the poem "The Men Who Don't Fit In" by Robert Service to
illustrate apostolic gifting. His life reads like an adventure novel
whose central character loved to push the boundaries of convention
and irritate those in authority. This all sounds very apostolic, even
though there is scant evidence that Service was a follower of Jesus.
I hope you can look past his gender exclusivity—he was born in the
nineteenth century.

There is a race of men who don't fit in
    A race that can't stay still;
So they break the hearts of kith and kin,
    And they roam the world at will.
They range the field and they rove the flood,
    And they climb the mountain's crest;
Theirs is the curse of the gypsy blood,
    And they don't know how to rest.

If they just went straight they might go far;
    They are strong and brave and true;
But they're always tired of the things that are,
    And they want the strange and new.
They say: "Could I find my proper groove,
    What a deep mark I would make!"
So they chop and change, and each fresh move
    Is only a fresh mistake.

When I use the poem, I usually amend the last two lines this way:

These are the men who don't fit in,
    For whom the world is too small a place.

CLINTON ON *APOSTOLIC*

A more technical and comprehensive treatment of apostolic gifting can be found in the work of J. Robert Clinton, and specifically in his volume on spiritual gifts (coauthored with Richard W. Clinton). I like their definition: "The gift of apostleship refers to a special leadership capacity to move with authority from God to create new ministry structures (sodalities and modalities) to meet needs and to develop and appoint leadership in these structures." [13] I would add to their definition, ". . . to primarily cross barriers such as culture, language, socioeconomic status and geographic distance for the sake of the gospel and the kingdom."

Clinton's typology is particularly useful as he grounds apostolic functions in a case study of Titus and Timothy. He summarizes by saying:

> Apostolic functions involve the critical job of expanding ministry into new situations. Without this expansion, Christianity would die. Apostles exhibit strong gifts and strong leadership. Along with this strength goes the corresponding weakness of independence. Interdependence is needed—especially for accountability. Most apostolic workers do not have accountability for their ministries and hence abuses of power and heresies, both orthodoxic and orthopraxic, occur.[14]

Clinton also points out that apostolic worker are strong, task-oriented individuals who may often lack much-needed relational skills. They are builders. They are pioneers. They have a passion for what could be and, accompanied by a gift of faith, they have the capacity for visualizing and actualizing the future against all odds. "Hats off to apostolic workers! They carry out the Great Commission. They want to reach the world!"[15]

CLINTON'S GUIDELINES

Clinton also offers practical help in what he calls his Six Major Guidelines for developing apostolic giftedness. They are worth repeating.[16]

1. *Study the Bible.* Someone with apostolic gifting needs to be an all-around student of the Bible. You need to especially focus on the passages that deal with the working of this gift: the pastoral epistles, the church epistles, leadership passages throughout the Bible, and the book of Acts. You basically need to know the bounds within which you will operate in introducing new works, appointing leaders and evaluating works for genuineness. You

need to study every apostolic function, such as Barnabas's evaluation of Christianity at Antioch, the Jerusalem council's evaluation of possible heresy, Titus's apostolic role in appointing leaders and training them, Timothy's role in correcting the problems in Ephesus, etc. Particularly focus on Paul's burden for multiplying churches, his passion to start and initiate new works, establishing leadership and problem solving.

2. *Study sodalities and modalities.* You should have a clear understanding of the nature of the church along with its purposes, functions and growth processes. You should also have a clear understanding of the nature of sodalities along with their purposes, functions and growth processes. You should understand how these two essential expressions of the church relate.

3. *Develop your leadership skills.*

   • how to think strategically and develop strategies

   • how to plan and implement a plan

   • what skills are needed as a change agent

   • expertise in situational leadership styles

   • how to inspire and motivate followers

   • mentoring skills

   • organizational skills

   • team-building skills

   • how to identify, challenge, recruit and develop emerging leaders

4. *Communication skills.* Depending on the specific ministry context, you need to develop the appropriate communicational skills for that situation. Most important is understanding how to motivate people via inspirational leadership.

5. *Learn from others.* Biographies of other leaders are a great source of learning regarding apostolic personalities. Try to observe and study others who have begun new works and pioneered. If possible, establish mentoring relationships with other similarly gifted people.

6. *Develop your own intimacy with God.* Those with apostolic gifting need a great deal of faith to operate effectively. Deep faith comes from a deep relationship with God. This kind of relationship needs to be cultivated intentionally. There needs to be a special attention given to hearing the voice of God, obedience to that voice and the demonstration of power that comes with that. Spiritual authority ought to become the prime power base. Remember, spiritual authority is the right to influence conferred upon a leader by followers because of their perception of the leader's spirituality. It is delegated from God in its essence but is manifest in the leader via three elements:

   • Experiential knowledge of God—his person, character, ways, purpose;

   • Godliness in character—the effects of knowing God personally result in a character which is God-like; and

   • Gifted power—the leader operates in ministry with an aura and with manifest results of the supernatural upon the giftedness set (natural abilities, acquired skills and spiritual gifts).

APOSTOLIC CONFLICTS

Of the functions listed in Ephesians 4, two have the built-in potential to be provocative and thus act as catalysts for conflict. Prophets, by their very nature, are confrontational. Whether in the Old Testament or in their New Testament roles, those with prophetic gifting will dust it up with others. Likewise, those with apostolic gifting can be the source of unrelenting conflict. It's inherent in their gifting. As the Robert Service poem suggests, such people are not "content with the things that are." They invariably upset the status quo and create waves.

An interesting biblical example can be seen in the events of Acts 9:26-31. Even with Barnabas's sponsorship, the followers of Jesus in Jerusalem "were all afraid of [Paul], not believing that he really was a disciple" (verse 26). That's understandable in light of Paul's history as a leader of the persecution against Jesus' followers. Nevertheless, the passage indicates that Paul attained some level of credibility and that he "moved about freely . . . speaking boldly in the name of the Lord" (verse 28). As a result, the Hellenistic Jews tried to kill him. To remedy the situation, the other brothers "took him down to Caesarea and sent him off to Tarsus" (verse 30).

Then there is an obscure little verse where Luke tells what happened after they managed to get Paul, this provocative apostolic leader, out of Jerusalem. "Then the church throughout Judea, Galilee and Samaria enjoyed a time of peace" (verse 31). Interesting—they got rid of the one who was stirring up all the trouble and things settled down. Such a dynamic is illustrative of the relationship between apostolic people and those within local congregational structures.

While Peter Wagner calls them "three peculiar attitudes" that apostolic leaders evidence, I think they are rather normal, and I've seen them over and over again:

> First, they [meaning leaders of well-functioning apostolic structures] think their task is the most important task in the Kingdom of God. They respect what others are doing, but they have experienced such an urgency to their call that they cannot imagine any other ministry as important as theirs.

That is why they can go at what they are doing with a passion, which far surpasses that of the ordinary leaders of the congregational structure or modality.

Second, they believe that they are the only ones doing the particular task well. Few say this in public because it would appear altogether immodest. They treat leaders of similar sodalities with great respect and refer to their works with careful diplomacy. But if they are good sodality leaders they believe in their hearts that their particular methodology is superior to others, and if they doubt for a moment that it might not be superior, they will take immediate steps to rectify the situation.

These two above attitudes, which are precisely what are necessary for excellence in performing the task, often get good sodality leaders in trouble. They tend to irritate the modality leaders and also other sodality leaders. To the degree they don't, they are usually less effective. But the modality leaders should not allow themselves to be irritated by this because they should maintain the broad vision and be the ones to see that such attitudes on the part of sodality leaders are ultimately helpful to the Kingdom of God.

The third attitude characteristic of good sodality leaders is a relatively low need for people. By this I mean that personally and psychologically they do not crave deep, long-term, heart-to-heart relationships with persons outside their immediate family. They know either consciously or subconsciously that to the degree they become personally involved with others they may lose the objectivity required to monitor their performance in accomplishing the task. It is always a temptation to get their eyes off the task and on people. This does not prevent some of them from spending the time with a few middle-management leaders and pouring their lives into them in a discipling relationship. But they do this only as they see that it facilitates the task.[17]

THE BLESSING OF BALANCE

Most of the people I know with strong pastoral and relational skills would cringe at Wagner's analysis. It seems so unsanctified and less than ideal. But in reality, it is hard to argue with it. It's simply true.

Norris is one of those guys. Built like a tank, he played football at Arizona State University and then had his day in the sun with the Pittsburgh Steelers before an injury ended his football career. After 9/11 he helped pioneer ministry in the Middle East that is resulting today in many thousands of people becoming committed, obedient followers of Jesus. After graciously transitioning leadership to national leaders, he capitalized on what he learned in that volatile region of the world and has gone on to train and catalyze movement leadership in places such as Russia, Nigeria, Venezuela and South Africa, all the while growing cherries on a farm in central Washington State. He's the type of guy I never want to run into in a dark alley at night, yet his eyes will tear up when he describes the gospel movements that are multiplying in such diverse cultural settings.

I know many apostolic leaders—Norris being one of them—who are criticized regularly as they live out these strong leadership traits. I too have been the object of the same response. Granted, some of the piling on may be justified. Every spiritual gift needs to be brought under the control of the Spirit of God and is subject to God's refining process in a person's life. But the church desperately needs these apostolic people if the momentum to catalyze and sustain movements of the gospel has any chance of succeeding.

At the same time, these apostolic leaders desperately need others with complementary gifts alongside them. For example, many such apostolic leaders can be a disaster administratively. They need those gifted to handle the details to ensure that money is spent well and that vision is undergirded with unquestionable integrity.

My wife—with her gifts of mercy and compassion—is greatly appreciated when she ministers in tandem with others who have the hard-charging tendencies that come with apostolic gifting. The running joke among those who work for me is that "Sam afflicts the comfortable and Patty comforts the afflicted!" Likewise, God has often seen fit to bring others around me who can complement who I am and fill in the gaps in my leadership that come from the limitations of my own giftedness. For me, this means often having people alongside who have pastoral gifts. They are the ones who soften my rough edges and bring relational ballast to my drive and determination.

So if you are one of these people with apostolic gifting, be encouraged. You have a vital and important role to play. Find your groove and "make your mark," as Robert Service admonishes. And as you do, may God bring alongside you those who can refine, complement and accelerate your unique contribution to the King and his kingdom.

Holy Discontent and Sanctified Ambition

The apostolic imperative of Ephesians 4

*If we consider the unblushing promises of reward and
the staggering nature of the rewards promised
in the Gospels, it would seem that our
Lord finds our desires not too
strong, but too weak.*

C. S. Lewis, *The Weight of Glory*

*"Apostolic passion," therefore, is a deliberate, intentional choice to
live for the worship of Jesus in the nations. It has to do with
being committed to the point of death to spreading
His glory. It's the quality of those who are on fire
for Jesus, who dream of the whole earth being
covered with the Glory of the Lord.*

Floyd McClung, "Apostolic Passion"

*Let others complain that the times are evil. I complain
that they are wretched, for they are without passion.*

Søren Kierkegaard, *Either/Or*

One of the keys to mobilizing people with apostolic calling is to identify those with holy discontent. Usually, I find it's a waste of time trying to motivate the unmotivated for the sake of apostolic ministry. If someone has to be motivated, then most likely apostolic gifting and calling are not part of their gift mix.

I find holy discontent most often among the underchallenged, those stuck in a maintenance role in an existing local church or in a ministry context that's a mismatch for their gifts and passion. I have sat across from countless young leaders who have been over-educated, underchallenged, and are going around and around in ministry cul-de-sacs, many with latent apostolic gifting just waiting for an outlet.

A second key that I look for is sanctified ambition. In the Christian world we often consider someone with ambition to be suspect. There is something secular or worldly about ambition that rubs us the wrong way. We've come to equate it with a lack of humility or an inability to depend on God. But when it is sanctified, ambition can be a powerful and wonderful thing. It's necessary for the health and vibrancy of the Christian movement.

Unfortunately, many very capable leaders are quashed because of other people's fear of the visionary. William Carey, the father of modern missions, was repeatedly discouraged and put in his place by the ecclesiastical authorities of the day when he tried to rekindle a missional fire in the English church. His famous dictum "expect great things from God, attempt great things for God" exudes such sanctified ambition. Or consider Hudson Taylor of the China Inland Mission, who said, "There are three stages to every great work of God: first it is impossible, then it is difficult, then it is done."

Younger leaders are particularly susceptible to disqualification at this crucial point. Too many have their spirits dampened by well-intentioned older leaders who simply cannot handle the unbridled passion of the next generation. An outstanding model of a leader who was *not* intimidated by apostolic passion is Barnabas in the book of Acts. Had it not been for Barnabas, we would never have had Paul.

When I was in my twenties, an older leader pulled me aside and asked me to do a study from the Scriptures about how Barnabas recruited and developed Paul. In other words, how did the "son of encouragement" corral and develop a much more charismatic, apostolic leader who would eventually surpass him in influence and leadership? It was a fascinating case study. I have drawn on those lessons many times in subsequent years when I've worked with passionate younger leaders who have the potential to be the William Careys or Hudson Taylors of their generation.

Doubtless the key in any time or context for making both discontent and ambition palatable is that the Spirit of God must sanctify them both. Such God-given drive must be made holy or it will be destructive. But that's no different from any other spiritual gift.

I wish I had known and understood these lessons in earlier years, rather than learning so much the hard way. Apostolic people can be very hard-headed—it's part of what makes them resilient and enables them to persevere. In my own journey, it took a variety of factors to form and shape me—a process that's still ongoing.

I had patient and understanding mentors. I was enfolded into an apostolic structure (a missionary organization) in my early twenties that provided a strong sense of community, discipline and vision. I was incubated as a follower, which is an indispensable prerequisite for leadership. I was encouraged to dream and imagine with God what *could be.* I was grounded in the Bible and basic spiritual disciplines that have lasted a lifetime. I was a member of teams where peers corrected, admonished and refined my character. And most important of all, I was simmered and seasoned in an environment where intimacy with Jesus and obedience to his call were the highest priorities.

One of my lifetime ambitions is to provide experiences like these for others, hopefully better designed because of my own failures. For example, I quietly created an opening for a "ministry assistant" who could travel with me and shadow me wherever I go. I've realized that for younger leaders, more is caught than is taught, and I can transfer more into someone's life at thirty thousand feet than in a classroom setting. These ministry assistants get the opportunity to see dozens of countries and crosscultural ministries and to experience apostolic, missionary life from the inside out. It is one of my most effective processes for passing the baton to the emerging generation.

I find that people with a sense of apostolic gifting and calling simply know it. It burns within them. It needs to be called out: to be blessed and released. I find great fulfillment in being a part of that process because I know that ultimately such men and women are key to making the name of Jesus renowned among the nations.

EPHESIANS 4

The taxonomy of Ephesians 4 is a necessary blueprint for the health and maturity of the church in all its forms. The church needs each of those referred to in this passage—Apostles, Prophets, Evangelists, Shepherds (pastors) and Teachers (APEST)—to be present and active. That's an exegetical and experiential given that I refuse to debate. The entire passage—verses 1 through 16—has universal application.

> As far as we can discern, it is simply not possible to be the church that Jesus intended if three (APE) of the five constitutional ministries are removed. According to the explicit teaching of Ephesians 4:1-16, it cannot be done. But in fact it has been done, and the tragic consequences are dramatically demonstrated in and through the history of the Christian church through the past seventeen centuries. . . . Every time we seem to develop some semblance of movement and get the

missional boulder up the hill, it rolls back down again, only to initiate the next cycle of seemingly futile efforts all over again. Seldom (and maybe never) have we stopped to correct our misunderstandings at this point.[1]

Throughout history there have been spurious theological arguments used to write off the A and P, and sometimes the E, functions. But I believe one of the primary reasons for the lack of understanding and application of APEST to its fullest in the whole church is structure. Without the necessary structures where these various roles can thrive appropriately, the typology is bound to fall short. Trying to shoehorn apostolically gifted people *only* into local church expressions is destined to result in the frustration that Hirsch and Catchim describe.

What this means is that our basic understanding of what the church is must be expansive enough not to limit APEST to the church in its local form. If we believe APEST can only—or must—be fully expressed in local, congregational, parish church expressions, that is, in modalities, then we will only continue this ongoing cycle of unmet expectations that has been repeated over and over throughout history. The missional boulder will continue to roll back down the hill. It is simply unrealistic to expect full expressions of this typology to exist in modalities. It just doesn't happen. The fundamental reason is we cannot put second decision people into first decision structures. Despite the understandable desire of some pastors and local church leaders to have everything within their own purview, such control will produce limited missional results.

So how does the APEST typology relate to structure? Specifically, how does APEST fit with the two-structures paradigm that missiologists advocate? First, we have to realize that all of these roles can and do function in modalities. But each of them can also be expressed in a sodality structure. So, while it is a "both/and" dynamic, the *proportions* of how the gifts are expressed in each of the structural components varies.

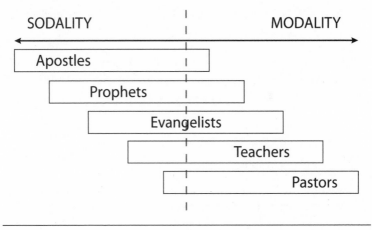

Figure 5.1

This diagram is not watertight, but it helps illustrate that certain of these gifts will be proportionally fulfilled most effectively in sodalities. Other roles, toward the right side of the chart, will more often be effectively expressed in modalities. That's an important technicality. What I am calling "apostolic structures" in this volume are sodalities led by apostolic people that uniquely accommodate the giftedness of those on the left side of the diagram.

APEST IN MODALITIES AND SODALITIES

When APEST functions in modalities, these gifts and gifted people will have certain distinct characteristics:

- Modalities are generalist structures. Thus these gifts and functions will be exercised broadly, non-selectively and to larger numbers of people.

- The boundaries and scope of APEST operating in modalities are most effective for "near-neighbors."

- When the APEST gifts are lived out in modalities, the ministry is carried out overwhelmingly by first decision people.

When APEST functions in sodalities, these gifts and gifted people will have a different set of characteristics:

- Sodalities are specialist structures. Thus the exercise of these gifts will have a single task and a narrow sense of calling. The gifts will be exercised intensely, since the sodality has the luxury of focus.

- The boundaries and scope of APEST operating in sodalities can be greater because sodalities are structured to cross cultural, social and geographic barriers.

- When the APEST functions are lived out in sodalities, the ministry is carried out primarily by second decision people. This sociological distinction cannot be underestimated.

Let's consider some examples. A teacher can certainly find room to exercise his or her giftedness in the context of a local church. Many of us know of attempts by pastors to embed a strong teaching ministry within their local church setting. Over the centuries, local churches have often shown a certain uneasiness toward formal and higher education, fearing that educational institutions are somehow co-opting functions that would be better placed in the local church context.

However, there are those for whom teaching has such a strong draw that they need to make the vocational jump—a second decision—to be in a ministry structure with others who have made a similar vocational commitment, and where their common calling as teachers can be more fully expressed. That is how we get schools, colleges and universities. There is no way that even the best and largest local church can duplicate or come close to the quality of these purely educational institutions. These institutions are actually educational sodalities. That's a sociological reality. They are sodalities where strong teaching gifts have the potential to flourish, even though educational institutions face their own difficulties with institutional inertia.

Prophetic gifting can and should be exercised in any local church expression. But when that prophetic function takes on a broader scope than "near-neighbor," and those exercising it make a vocational choice as second decision people, the gifting is best lived out in a sodality. For example, those called to serve vocationally with International Justice Mission, headquartered in Washington, DC, live out a clear prophetic ministry in a sodality. As a leading human rights agency, IJM rescues victims of slavery, sexual exploitation and other forms of violent oppression and works with local officials around the world to ensure that public justice systems protect victims of injustice.

Does that mean that local churches should not be concerned or committed to social justice or to issues of human trafficking or religious persecution? Of course not. But there is no local church— or even megachurch—that can begin to match the expertise and focus of International Justice Mission. The singular task of IJM, the expertise of its people and the global scope of its work are all far beyond the purview of any local modality expression. It's like the story of Diane in chapter four. It takes a structure with a scope and diversity that goes beyond the local church to catalyze a ministry among prostitutes in Cambodia, create an AIDS hospice, pioneer work among the poor in Romania and lead missionary teams all over the world.

Or let's consider the role of the evangelist in the APEST typology. Those gifted as evangelists should certainly be able to exercise their gift in their own church settings, especially if the scope of that ministry is near-neighbor. Harnessing that APEST function is essential if any local church is to flourish and have a redemptive impact.

But the further we move from that local expression—either in culture, language, socioeconomic status or geography—the more a sodality is needed. The Billy Graham Evangelistic Association and the Luis Palau Association are examples of sodalities that have an evangelistic focus. Similarly, Campus Crusade for Christ—now called Cru—is a sodality with evangelism as its primary focus. No local church expression or denomination anywhere in the world is capable of what Cru does, either in its specific focus or the magnitude of its impact, nor would that be a reasonable expectation.

While my focus in this book is on the apostolic aspect of the APEST typology, a similar case could be made for each of the APEST functions in Ephesians 4. It is not uncommon to see people in pastoral roles leave their local church positions, begin a sodality and focus their lives and ministry on one narrow, specialized work that carries out one specific aspect of APEST. They may need to be released from the general demands of leading a local modality in order to focus their calling and work vocationally alongside other second decision people.

FROM LOCAL TO SODAL

Approximately 30 percent of those who serve with CRM come to us after working on the staff of a local church. That's because many of them intuitively realized they are sodality people. They are people craving the commitment of a second decision and a place where their second decision can be validated and affirmed. Because their gifts cannot be adequately fulfilled in a local congregation, a different—yet equally legitimate—expression of the church is needed for them to live out God's calling on their lives.

- Bryan had been a youth pastor for eight years before making the jump to become a missionary. He was first sent to Australia to train and develop church planters down under but now lives in North America where he is one of the best church planting coaches in the eastern United States.

- Bill and Jill were pastors who had struggled valiantly for years to see their church on the west coast of the United States—and their denomination as a whole—recognize and infuse ministries of physical healing and the supernatural. Now they have moved on to an itinerant, apostolic role in a sodality, where they are free to do such training broadly and internationally.

- David had been through several pastorates in the southeastern United States. Now he leads a team that coaches and "pastors pastors" throughout North America.

- After attending seminary together and getting married, Dave and Kim served in pastoral ministry, but soon found they didn't really fit. They now live in the interior of China and carry on a robust leadership coaching ministry that has far-reaching results all across Asia.

All these are superbly gifted men and women who just needed a different context—beyond the local church—in which to thrive.

THE FLEXIBILITY OF APEST

The continuum in the chart above (Figure 5.1) is a generalization, and the APEST typology is not rigid. It is possible to have different combinations of gifts, so that a teacher, for example, who needs to be in a sodality structure, may also have apostolic gifting. Because of this secondary gifting, such a person will probably find more fulfillment in a teaching assignment that is crosscultural, pioneering and radical in its demands.

Certainly there are examples of people with a strong apostolic calling who choose to work in and through local church expressions. Many megachurch leaders in North America are people with an apostolic calling who have chosen to use a local church structure as a base for living out their ministry. Some do it because of their convictions regarding the local church. Others do it out of pragmatism—

they're willing to sacrifice some freedom and flexibility in order to gain access to the resources of the local church body, resources that are inherently greater than what's commonly found in sodalities.

Also, in any good apostolic sodality, there is room for a few—not many—shepherds and teachers. Every army needs a hospital. Every Navy SEAL team needs an instructor. But it helps if those so gifted *also* have an apostolic gift as a secondary element of their giftedness set. At the very least, they need to have an appreciation of apostolic sodalities and how their pastoral calling can make a unique contribution within them. Without it, these people can be quite conflicted. I've seen it often. These are the individuals who move back and forth between local church roles and specialized ministry roles beyond the church, never really content in one or the other.

Though I was not an insider to the Vineyard movement during the last two decades of the twentieth century, I believe this was part of the dynamic that the movement's leader, John Wimber, experienced. Wimber had clear apostolic gifting. He oozed it. He wisely started a movement that had all sorts of sodality appendages around it—Vineyard Ministries International, Vineyard Music and so on, and his calling was international in scope—much broader than one local congregation.

On the other hand, he was also a pastor at heart. He found it difficult to extricate himself from hands-on involvement at the local level, as a shepherd relationally connected to people. So consequently he was pulled back and forth from one structure to the other in the continuum above (figure 5.1). As an outsider, my observation is that the movement had a difficult time accommodating Wimber's vocational schizophrenia.

As a general rule, the continuum in figure 5.1 holds true. I've seen it in the West, in globalized cities on every continent and in rural and developing areas of the majority world. It spans cultures and socioeconomic distinctions as well.

We also know that APEST—and particularly the APE functions—can be sadly misunderstood and deemphasized in the church in the West. I like the way Hirsch and Catchim illustrate this imbalance in the following diagram.[2]

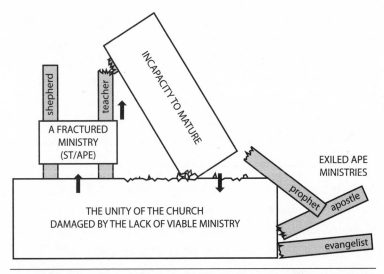

Figure 5.2. From Alan Hirsch and Tim Catchim, *The Permanent Revolution* (San Francisco: Jossey-Bass, 2012), p. 17.

Consequently, apostles, prophets and evangelists may not be well represented or utilized in either modalities or sodalities. When that happens, the entire church is impoverished.

> In relation to those unaware, yet not-yet convinced, or even those who harbor antipathy towards the idea of the fivefold ministry in general and the apostolic in particular, our aim is nothing less than to get you to change your mind about the importance of these for the church in our day. We cannot shake the conviction that nothing less than the future viability of the Western church is somehow involved in the revitalization of its ministry along more biblical lines.[3]

PAULINE AND PETRINE APOSTOLIC LEADERS

A helpful biblical distinction can be made between two different types
of apostolic leaders: Pauline and Petrine. Dick Scoggins describes it
this way:

> Pauline apostleship is exercised by pioneering, mobile com-
> munities which start local communities of the Kingdom
> where they do not exist. . . . A second form of apostleship—
> what I would call Petrine apostleship—is also portrayed in the
> New Testament . . . [and] is much more prevalent than I had
> imagined. . . . There is an apostolic ministry to the unreached
> (the Pauline), but there is also an apostolic ministry to the
> existing people of God (the Petrine).[4]

Scoggins goes on to ground his understanding of Petrine apostleship in Galatians 2:8-10, where Peter gives legitimacy to Paul and
Barnabas and their calling, and Paul and Barnabas likewise return
the commendation by recognizing Peter's (and James's and John's)
calling to the circumcised, that is, the already-existing people of
God. Hirsch and Catchim also describe this distinction.

> In modern equivalents of apostolic ministry in Western con-
> texts, the Pauline is called to extend and establish Christianity
> onto new ground in the West, while the Petrine is called to
> help reframe the nature of Western Christianity itself. The one
> form is thus primarily pioneering and crosscultural and the
> other innovative and intracultural.[5]
>
> Whereas Pauline apostles tend to cross cultures to pioneer
> new missional communities, Petrine apostles tend to mobilize
> existing communities to become and remain missional.[6]

Hirsch and Catchim devote an entire chapter entitled "Come
Back Peter, Come Back Paul" to these two apostolic functions. It
is an excellent overview, but there are some additional implica-

tions to be drawn from this distinction when it's applied to structures.

First, when a sodality person ministers alongside a modality, Petrine apostolic giftedness can probably be more easily tolerated than Pauline giftedness. Even so, Petrine apostolic people can still be an irritant. Though the focus of Petrine giftedness is the existing church and what "is," rather than the type of extreme, out-of-the-box ministry typical of Pauline giftedness, Petrine types can appear to be forcing a blessing down the throats of local church and denominational leaders. If local churches are the beneficiaries of Petrine efforts, responsive congregational leaders will be needed, with a sense of vision beyond their own local church, an understanding of their limitations and a willingness to access and receive outside help. Sensitivity and maturity will also be needed from those exercising Petrine apostolicity.

Second, vibrant local congregations should always be looking to recruit and include good Petrine leaders internally. The challenge for those Petrine leaders comes when they become insiders in a modality. If they are financially dependent on it, they run the risk of being co-opted by the system. Freedom can be traded for security.

I recently met with Matt, a young leader with very obvious Petrine apostolic abilities. He's presently working for a mission organization—an apostolic sodality—and is being actively courted by a large megachurch in our area to fill a pastoral staff position. Initially, the job was attractive to him. Matt has a young family and the megachurch offers a stable salary. On paper, it looked challenging enough and seemed like a good fit for his gifts and sense of calling.

But during the courting process things began to change. The role began to morph almost weekly, and each time it was altered, the

apostolic nature of the job description shrunk a little bit. It slowly
eroded into a maintenance role, ministering to existing church
members with little to no missional focus. Matt's fear was that once
he got on the inside, he would be swamped by pastoral needs and
any apostolic drive would be compromised and controlled. So Matt
turned the job down, realizing that his contribution to this congregation can be better made by serving alongside the church, rather
than inside it.

Serving alongside, as opposed to inside, a modality has distinct
advantages and can contribute to a healthier dynamic in which apostolic presence can be more effective. Being an outsider can free
Petrine apostles to speak more prophetically and honestly than if
they were on the inside, and consequently they can exercise a
greater degree of influence.

CRM's ReTurn team is comprised of experienced, mature people
with Petrine apostolic gifts who focus on churches and congregations in dire straits—churches that are in the ER and need inter-
vention or they will die. And if they do die, the ReTurn team knows
how to help them die with dignity.

Our ReTurn staff are trained to come alongside such churches in
crisis and, as Paul wrote to Titus, "put in order what was left unfin-
ished" (Titus 1:5). They have successfully done this in congregation
after congregation. One of the keys to their effectiveness has been
their choice to remain formally alongside the churches they serve,
and not be financially dependent on them. This enables them to be
more honest brokers of change.

Third, those with a Pauline apostolic call need structures designed to work and minister across cultural, linguistic, socioeconomic and geographical barriers—that is, structures that are missionary in nature. Working internationally or crossculturally brings
enormous additional challenges in the contemporary world, which
require entities uniquely designed to tackle them.

COMBINING PETER, PAUL AND JOHN

There can be combinations of Pauline and Petrine apostolic ministry. For example, there are people with Pauline apostolic gifts who will live and work crossculturally, even though their function in that crosscultural setting is more Petrine. We have numerous missionaries serving with our organization who work to strengthen existing churches in crosscultural settings. They are not necessarily pioneering new ground in a Pauline manner.

Jim Creasman has done this for years. After living and learning language in the interior of China, Jim and his family moved to Singapore. From there, he carried on a mentoring/coaching ministry among pastors and church leaders that has made a substantive contribution to the Christian movement in numerous nations throughout Southeast Asia. Or consider Brad Baker, who in his twenties moved to Hungary from the United States while Eastern Europe was still under communism. Today, he is a missionary statesman, fluent in the language, and has a highly leveraged ministry among multiple Hungarian churches that emerged from this dark chapter of the twentieth century.

I can point to many other men and women like Jim and Brad, in dozens of countries, who have crosscultural skills and can move with ease across cultural, linguistic and social barriers for the sake of mission, but whose focus is Petrine in nature, ministering tirelessly alongside and among existing local churches.

Interestingly, there have been some discussions among missiologists about a third apostolic function, called Johannine (named after the apostle John). While the biblical evidence is less compelling and more speculative, the distinction is intriguing. People with a Johannine apostolic gift are those highly relational individuals who excel in loving and caring for others. However, they often have a built-in aversion to structure and little organizational or strategic sense. They break out in hives when inspirational or task-oriented leadership trumps the relational. But they love people intensely and bring balance and heart to ministry.

For example, at CRM we have a specialized team—our SDCT (Staff Development and Care Team)—with a dozen people committed to the development, care and nurture of our personnel around the world. Our SDCT includes therapists, counselors, spiritual directors and so on, all of whom are highly relational and expertly trained. It's full of people with Johannine apostolic abilities. With the enormous amount of time and resources invested in finding and deploying high quality Pauline and Petrine apostles all over the world, we want to minimize the casualties. Stewarding our people is a high value, and this team is designed to do that. They are invaluable.

Another place where the exercise of strong Johannine apostolic giftedness comes into play is in sodalities focused on ministries of mercy. I suspect that's true of Mother Teresa's Sisters of Mercy, a sodality where there is a combination of strong apostolic gifts *and* mercy. There are many relief and development agencies where the Johannine apostolic calling can flourish.

The normal pattern is for Pauline, Petrine or Johannine apostles to gravitate toward sodality structures that reflect these particular distinctions. However, two or all three of these functions can exist under the umbrella of the same apostolic sodality. If they do, there may well be tensions, no different than the tensions that flared between Paul and Peter or Paul and Barnabas.

When these three kinds of apostolically gifted people coexist in the same entity, they can each bring much-needed strengths to organizational leadership. For example, those with Pauline apostolic gifting will tend to be the most radical. They will force the structure to stay focused on their task and to push the boundaries of calling, keeping everyone on the margins and pushing to the frontiers. Those with Petrine gifting will consolidate, build infrastructure and increase apostolic capacity. And those with Johannine gifting will contribute to the quality of life together and hence the quality of the ministry being multiplied in the world. All three play an important part.

LIVING ON THE EDGE

As classic edge people, apostles are at the forefront of extending Christianity into new situations. As seeders of the DNA of God's people, they are directly associated with the mission of the church and are keen to ensure that the message is transmitted from one culture to another. They have to be innovators and entrepreneurs because what works in one context might not necessarily work in another. . . . The missional ministry of the apostolic person is vital not only for the extension of Christianity to new ground but also to maintaining the health of the home base was well.[7]

As I described at the beginning of chapter two, I've stood on the shore of Iona, the island off the west coast of Scotland from which missionaries fanned out to evangelize all of Scotland and many other lands of Western Europe. Founded by St. Columba in AD 563, the abbey at Iona was a catalytic missional force in the British Isles for centuries, exuding passion, fervency and great spiritual power.

Reading between the lines in the historical accounts, such as Adomnán of Iona's *Life of St. Columba*, it is clear that Columba operated with apostolic calling and authority.[8] He also demonstrated a prophetic gift and moved comfortably in the supernatural realm, whether through healings, dealing with demons or discerning the presence of angels.

Columba had the message, he had the means and he mastered the mechanics of apostolic ministry. And with his band of Celtic sojourners he had the necessary apostolic structure. Today the broader culture in Britain and throughout Europe is ripe for a re-birth of such apostolic fervency.

I've met and worked with present day Columbas in urban set-tings such as London and Glasgow. I've seen teams of contem-porary Celt-like missionaries committed to re-evangelizing Britain. These apostolic teams are remarkably similar in values and phi-losophy of ministry to their brothers and sisters of fifteen centuries ago. I've watched younger British believers be captivated by the compelling vision of these teams and regain their mojo for effective evangelism and discipleship in the midst of secular postmodernity.

May God multiply apostles in our own time in the mold of St. Columba in Scotland, St. Patrick in Ireland and Aidan in England across the globe and beyond the local church, and may their move-ments proliferate. May the Spirit of God release multitudes of those with holy discontent and sanctified ambition to live out more fully the rich diversity of Ephesians 4, and through them "remonk" the church in this generation.

6

Setting Visionaries Free

Pioneering as a second decision entrepreneur

*The sodal is distinctly vocational; a call that will be
tested by others, and in that sense it is exclusive.
Not everyone can join or should.*

George Lings, "Why Modality and Sodality Thinking
Is Vital to Understand Future Church"

*The Jesuits carry the reputation of clerical commandos. In the
US Army, a Green Beret can't rise above the rank of colonel.
That's because men trained to freelance as fighters aren't likely
to fit well in the command-and-control system of the Army. The
Catholic Church has drawn a similar conclusion about the order
that Ignatius of Loyola founded in 1534. What makes for creative
and effective witness on the frontiers of Christianity usually isn't
what's needed for the daily running of the institutional church.*

R. R. Reno

first saw a print of the painting *The Missionary's Adventures* hanging in the School of World Mission at Fuller Theological Seminary. I was intrigued, so I tracked it down and discovered that the original was in the Metropolitan Museum of Art in New York City. Painted by Jehan Georges Vibert (1840–1902), it is a powerful visual representation of the dynamic between apostolic people and indifferent ecclesiological structures.

Figure 6.1. *The Missionary's Adventures* **by Jehan Georges Vibert (public domain)**

The setting is opulent. In the center, leaning into the conversation, is a friar. We know who he is by the way he's dressed. He's pointing to scars in his hand, probably received during whatever missionary journey he's just returned from. Two of the cardinals aren't even listening, but are carrying on a side conversation. The others look skeptical or disinterested, and the rotund bishop on the far right is partaking of the refreshments available from the silver tea set.

The painting drips with irony. In the right hand corner, a dog sits on its hind legs begging for crumbs from the master's table, a strong biblical image that brings to mind Jesus' own words about dogs eating scraps from a table. The whole scene takes place under the gaze of another painting, which could not be more poignant. Although difficult to see, on the wall to the left hangs José de Ribera's famous painting *The Martyrdom of Saint Bartholomew*, which illustrates the torture and execution of the apostle Bartholomew. The contrast between that reality and the deadening poshness of the setting it overlooks could not be more striking.

The contrast between the modality that has lost its way and the sodality speaking prophetically to the ecclesiastical powers is poignant. It is pregnant with meaning. I am reminded of the famous story of the pope giving Thomas Aquinas a tour of the Vatican. The pope told Aquinas, "It is obvious that the church can no longer say, 'Silver and gold have I none,'" to which Aquinas is supposed to have replied, "Neither can she say, 'In the name of Jesus, stand up and walk.'"

THE SECOND DECISION DISTINCTIVE

Perhaps one of the most significant factors that distinguishes sodalities from modalities is that that sodalities are made up of second decision people. First decision people are those who make the decision to follow Jesus and are part of some form of the local church—a modality. Second decision people are those who make an additional vocational commitment to a specialized ministry that is made up of people like themselves who have made similar vocational choices.

This sociological distinction between first and second decision people allows sodalities to do three unique things. First, they can enforce discipline. It's hard to imagine discipline in a local church being exercised in ways St. Benedict prescribes in the famous *Rule of St. Benedict,* one of the models for orders throughout the monastic tradition. While Benedict admonishes those serving as abbots to be holy and lead with love and equanimity, he also empowers them to exercise discipline with a firm hand over those in their charge. In chapter two he writes, "But those who are evil or stubborn, arrogant or disobedient, he [the abbot] can curb only by blows or some other physical punishment at the first offense. It is written, 'The fool cannot be corrected with words,' and again 'Strike your son with a rod and you will free his soul from death.'"[1]

Second, sodalities have the authority to move people in and out. Because a second decision is a vocational choice, sodalities have the leverage to enforce discipline by removing people. If a monk or a nun does not live up to the common rule, he or she can be dismissed. If a Young Life staffer, a YWAM missionary or a translator with Wycliffe Bible Translators exhibits behavior inconsistent with the ministry's values, beliefs, calling or expectations, the organization can let them go.

Third, sodalities can maintain a long, vibrant organizational life cycle. In his study of the cycles of renewal in organizations, J. Robert Clinton estimates that the typical life cycle of a local church in the Western world is five generations, before nominalism or apostasy sets in.[2] It can be difficult—as anyone who has ever been involved in church discipline in a local church setting can attest—to maintain standards with volunteers. Sodalities, on the other hand, are not made up of volunteers, which is an inherent difference between first and second decision commitments. Discipline is easier to enforce and therefore sodalities can maintain their vibrancy for much longer.

A VOCATIONAL CHOICE

Sodalities provide a *vocational* place for people with a second decision calling to live and minister with people similarly called. "There is also a difference about the joining patterns; the modal tends toward the self-inclusive; you join if you want to. The sodal is distinctly vocational, a call that will be tested by others, and in that sense, it is exclusive. Not everyone can join or should."[3]

This can be problematic for those who are not keen on people in professional or vocational ministry or who uncritically advocate the priesthood of all believers, one of the foundational mantras of the Protestant Reformation. Believing that we are in (or should be in) a new "age of the laity" is a perspective that periodically sweeps through the greater Christian movement. But if we look at it closely, there should be no conflict between these values and second decision calling properly understood. Both are necessary and complementary.

The concept of people being set aside for vocational ministry is clearly evident throughout the Scriptures. The Levites were the priestly class and were specifically set aside for ministry in Israel. So were the prophets. The same is true for those ministering throughout the Old Testament, described in chapter one. This pattern continues into the New Testament.

While Jesus initially worked at a trade, his public ministry, begun at age 30, was a full-time vocation, and he and his disciples lived off of the generosity and gifts of others. It is hard to argue with the clear passages in Paul's epistles (1 Corinthians 9, 2 Corinthians 8–9) that describe and justify people who are called into vocational ministry. And it is a strong statement that "the Lord has commanded that those who preach the gospel should receive their living from the gospel" (1 Corinthians 9:14).

The posture of living and working vocationally is not limited to those who pastor or shepherd local churches. As Paul explains, those who have made the move into apostolic ministry in a sodality are equally valid recipients of people's giving. We see that in Scripture. It is also a logical deduction if we embrace the reality that sodalities are just as much a part of the church as modalities.

FUNDING APOSTOLIC WORKERS

Fundraising is one of the primary means God has designed for the support of his work and of those called to minister in apostolic sodalities. There are some excellent books available on the topic. Scott Morton's *Funding Your Ministry* is a good resource, along with *Viewpoints* and *The God Ask* by Steve Shadrach.[4] More can be found at cmmpress.org. Some general principles of funding include:

1. Our giving should not be limited or relegated to the church in its local form.

2. Giving to local churches does not take priority over giving to sodalities. There should be no difference. The local church doesn't get "tithes" while sodalities get "offerings." It comes down—again—to our definition of *church*. If our definition includes both modalities and sodalities, then both are worthy recipients of our stewardship.

3. The biblical admonition regarding our giving priorities is to give first to those ministries that minister to us personally (Galatians 6:6). They can be either modalities or sodalities.

LIVING ON "SUPPORT"

I appreciate Michael Frost and Alan Hirsch's observation about funding for ministry in the contemporary world when they write that "mission support . . . is the support system of the future. . . . Sustainability and organic growth are at stake."[5]

My wife, Patty, and I have lived off support for four decades, meaning we have raised the necessary funds for our salary, expenses and benefits through the generous gifts of friends, family, churches and others among whom we have ministered. Recently I wrote about this to our friends and colleagues who serve with us around the world. "There have certainly been ups and downs—

times of plenty and times of want (Philippians 4:11-12). While we have never failed to see God's faithfulness in meeting our needs, there have been seasons when financial fatigue has set in."

I have heard all the excuses and justifications that argue that such support-raising is passé, and I've come up with some of my own at times, when the belt has been cinched particularly tight. But the validity of this funding paradigm remains, and I believe it offers two major strengths for second decision people.

First, raising and living off support reinforces a person's call to vocational ministry, particularly if that ministry is apostolic in nature and in an apostolic structure. The process can serve as a means for God to validate that calling. The challenge to trust God for such tangible needs is often a harbinger of the faith challenges that await those committed to living out an apostolic calling.

Second, the process can be a powerful tool in helping those who partner with us to make significant decisions about their resources. Particularly in the North American church, what people do with their resources may be one of the most important lordship decisions they will ever make. Asking people for financial support is *never* begging. Rather it is helping people determine, before God, what he would have them do with what he has entrusted to them. It is providing an opportunity for followers of Jesus to respond with generosity to God's leading.

IS SUPPORT THE ONLY WAY?

So is the support paradigm the *only* way to financially sustain those in vocational ministry? Of course not. Nor is it the only way it happened in the Bible. There are a variety of factors and combinations that have to be taken into consideration, and the computations become more complex—but no less valid—in crosscultural settings, among minority communities and in settings without a culture of giving. But there are ways to creatively provide sustainable funding, regardless of the context. Business as Mission (and Business *for* Mission) is one way business ventures can be used for ministry purposes and to provide complementary revenue streams.

The ministry I lead has been involved in numerous creative Business as Mission (BAM) efforts around the world, giving people with business education and skills tremendous opportunities to utilize their talents for kingdom purposes. Some have succeeded. Some have failed (and failed spectacularly). Regardless, we continue to invest resources and people in such efforts, believing they can make a significant contribution to God's worldwide plans and purposes.[6]

However, we cannot use alternative means of funding to diminish biblical examples and injunctions about the right of those who minister to benefit tangibly from the results of their labor.

Unfortunately, there are those who grow weary of living in such a posture. In my experience, sometimes these people have not worked hard enough at this process. They have failed to realize that helping supporters make stewardship decisions before God is an ongoing part of ministry. They have failed to see fundraising as an integral and essential aspect of apostolic ministry.

When the financial woes mount, some unfortunately give up. Some gravitate toward tentmaking. Some seek fees for services. Others come to believe raising money is too great an obstacle to overcome, and blame changing cultural demographics or the unwillingness of the local church in their context to give. Still others believe they have run out of potential donors in their circle of relationships. The reasons—and excuses—are many. I've made them myself.

An organization that I have found very helpful for getting one's head around this subject has been the Center for Mission Mobilization (mobilization.org). They do an excellent job of training people in the practical how-tos of raising support for ministry and in demythologizing many of the excuses and the emotional thinking that can surround the topic. There are other similar organizations as well, which train people to raise money crossculturally in the majority world, where cultural distinctives require adaptability and contextualization. One example is the Stewardship organization in the UK.[7]

Fundamentally, raising money is an exercise in spiritual formation. Few articulate this better than Henri Nouwen in his book *A Spirituality of Fundraising*, where he writes, "Fundraising is, first and foremost, a form of ministry. It is a way of announcing our vision and inviting other people into our mission. . . . Fundraising is proclaiming what we believe in such a way that we offer other people an opportunity to participate with us in our vision and mission."[8]

WHAT ABOUT TENTMAKING?

A concept that routinely comes in and out of vogue in the world of ministry is tentmaking. Derived from the biblical example of the apostle Paul, who made tents to make ends meet (Acts 18:3), the concept of tentmaking can be appealing as an alternative or complementary means of funding people who want to make a vocational transition to ministry.

Tentmaking certainly has a place in God's overall missional purposes around the world. There are many people who have made such crosscultural jumps and who serve, with great effectiveness, as representatives of Jesus through their jobs in difficult crosscultural contexts. But there needs to be some realism and honesty about what tentmaking can and cannot accomplish.

First, the biblical example of Paul making tents is not presented as the ideal. Paul does this because of the immaturity of the Corinthian church. He is clear that he has the right to expect their financial support, but he forgoes that right so as not to burden them in their embryonic developmental stage (1 Corinthians 9:7-18). Tentmaking is the default posture, not the norm.

Second, the limitations of tentmakers are usually substantial, and those undertaking tentmaking should have clear expectations of what they are pursuing. It is difficult to carry on a vocation or profession at forty-sixty hours per week in the midst of significant crosscultural stress and adjustments. Often little energy or time is realistically left for effective ministry. This means that the primary—sometimes the only—ministry context in which tentmakers can reasonably expect to function will be their tentmaking job.

ABSORBING SODALIC FUNCTIONS

Sometimes I'm asked if it's possible for sodalic functions to be more intentionally included or embedded in modalities. It's a question I occasionally get when interacting with pastors—particularly those who long for their people to be more missionally engaged. I believe the answer is "yes," but with some qualifiers, because modalic structures have some inherent limitations.

It is always the ideal that the spiritual vitality characteristic of apostolic structures flows over into local churches. I want to see local congregations adopt the strengths and expertise that sodalities, and especially apostolic sodalities, have to offer as much as local churches are able to absorb them. That has been the observable pattern for two thousand years. For example, in the Roman Catholic Church, renewal, vision and spiritual vitality have routinely flowed from the orders and religious communities into the greater Catholic Church. That's the historical reality and it's a wonderful dynamic.

The same has been true in the Eastern church, albeit with an interesting twist that has greatly contributed to spiritual vibrancy over the centuries. In the Orthodox tradition, parish priests are not promoted via the ecclesiological hierarchy to become bishops. Instead, bishops in the Eastern church are drawn from the monasteries. This process of populating the ecclesiastical leadership structure has had a pronounced effect. Spiritual fervor and vibrancy have been given a formalized, institutional pathway from the sodalities back into the modalities.

What really needs to flow into modalities is the *ethos* of sodalities, not their structure. It's the function, not the form. The reality is that spiritual vitality will wane faster in a modality because of its God-given structure. The things that give a modality purpose are the very things that shorten its shelf life. That's one of the reasons for the necessary relationship and interdependency between modalities and sodalities. The moment a modality decides to become a sodality, its mission and ministry to the masses will be more narrowly focused and compromised. A sodality will focus on the few within its clearly defined purpose and rarely the broad welfare of the many, even though many may benefit in the long run.

Such task-oriented, laser-like vision is the genius of the sodality, and particularly the apostolic sodality. As Robert Coleman puts it, "Victory is never won by the multitudes. . . . This principle of selectivity and concentration is engraved in the universe, and will bring results no matter who practices it, whether or not the church believes it."[9]

THE TWO-WAY STREET

Absorbing sodalic functions into modalities is an organizational dynamic that has been attempted for centuries. In our day some megachurches and denominational movements attempt to do it, often via internships, training programs or quasi-educational arrangements. But the effectiveness of such efforts has always been dependent on making a clear distinction between modality and sodality structures. Too often this distinction gets blurred. It needs to be reflected structurally and reinforced regularly. The clearer the distinction, the more effective the outcome. What Jesus did with the multitudes was different from what he did with the Twelve. While integrated, the two approaches were clearly different.

This partnership and cooperation ought to be undertaken in such a way that apostolic leaders and functions are given adequate freedom. The more freedom and autonomy are given to apostolic leaders, the more effective they will be.

Conversely, a pastoral concern ought to flow from local congregations into apostolic, missionary structures. It is common for apostolic people and structures to become so task oriented and mission obsessed that people get chewed up in the process. It's an observable phenomenon on the mission fields of the world—people are often used up and spent. Just like in an army, there needs to be adequate care for the troops. Every army needs a hospital. But the army is not the hospital. The moment the pastoral takes over, the army ceases to be an army. The purpose changes.

I'M NOT THE INNKEEPER

I was in a conversation about this dynamic with Tim, a young leader who was part of an intentional community living in an American inner city. Tim's community was determined to maintain high standards for those who were members, and in many ways it leaned toward being a sodality. But the community refused to make clear distinctions between first and second decision people, and incorporated a variety of other modality distinctives.

Over a period of years, the community and its members were continually pulled back and forth between the two structures and could never figure out exactly which they really were. They didn't know any differently, and they were confused. It was a textbook case of a ministry that could not determine whether it was "fish or fowl" and the resulting schizophrenia was detrimental to the community, its people and its mission. It was discouraging to see such gifted men and women flounder because they didn't understand these basic missiological concepts. The result was wasted time and energy.

Finally, in one of my conversations with Tim, there was a breakthrough. He used the parable of the Good Samaritan as a template through which to view his reality. "I've finally figured it out," he said, "and this parable illustrates it for me. I'm really the Good Samaritan on the road. That is what I do. Focused. Episodic. I am *not* the inn-keeper." That realization was a turning point, at least for Tim.

CALLED TO STAY NEAR

There will always be a need for those willing to go, pay the emotional and spiritual price, learn a language if need be and live incarnationally among the people to whom God has called them. There is no substitute for such commitment, no proxy to "staying near."

There is also a place for short-term mission experiences. I've written about this in a booklet, *Short-Term Missions: The Good, the Bad and the Ugly*, which is a more detailed treatment of this topic.[10] Short-term experiences rightly conceived and executed can play a beneficial and complementary role to those who are committed for the long haul. But short-term mission experiences will never replace the value or the necessity of a long-term incarnational presence.

In the years before and after the fall of communism, I spent much time in the former Soviet Union. My family and I lived briefly in Ukraine, and in their unguarded moments Russians and others in the Eastern Bloc would privately tell us, "If you really love us, come learn our language, live among us and serve." They were disenchanted with the short-term blitz approach from the West, which in many settings did more damage than good.

That is similar to what I heard in 2011 when I was in Iraq in a city of eight hundred thousand people, of which maybe three hundred were known followers of Jesus. Conversations with the leaders of this remnant were sobering. What these Iraqi leaders transparently shared was revealing. "We don't need any more seminars, conferences or experts coming in and out from the West telling us what to do. We are inundated with these people and their 'next best things.' We are fed up with that. Where are the people willing to live and die with us?"

The bottom line is that second decision people are desperately needed all over the world. The effects on the world of Mother Teresa and a few hundred fellow sisters is exponentially greater than hundreds of thousands of sacramentalized Roman Catholics. It is no different in the Protestant world. There will always be a need for those who will go (Matthew 28:19), crossing cultural, language and geographic barriers and "staying near" those they serve (Acts 8:29).

Libby and her husband, Tom, exemplified this truth when they lived and served in Afghanistan for over thirty years. Tom, a medical doctor, was one of a group of ten relief workers who were ambushed and murdered in the summer of 2010 by the Taliban about one hundred and fifty miles north of Kabul. In a riveting, sobering address at the Urbana conference a decade earlier, Libby described such commitment to an audience of twenty thousand students, not knowing that her husband would make the ultimate sacrifice in the years to come.

Our family was called to Afghanistan and we were called to "stay near." I am trembling here before you not from the frightening things that we have experienced living in a war zone, but I am trembling as I recall the times that God called us to stay and not leave the place of suffering. It was a place that we found God longing by his Holy Spirit to communicate his mercy and his lovingkindness to those who suffer.

During the next fifteen years of civil war, two of our team members were murdered. Colleagues were tortured. Our homes were hit with rockets. The hospital where my husband worked was completely destroyed. The front line of battle moved to our neighborhood streets. Weeks were filled with dragging the wounded and dying from collapsed buildings, rounding up terrified children and taking them to safety. There were robberies, attempted rapes, beatings and threats to our fellow team members. Perhaps for me, as the mother of three daughters, the hardest part of staying was trusting God daily for the safety of our children.

I confess I often wanted to escape the seriousness and sadness of war. Each of us knows that obedience to God does not mean immunity from suffering. "Staying near" may mean injury and even loss of life. We believe Jesus would say that in his kingdom, there are things worth dying for.

At a time when short mission trips are quite popular you might consider long-term service. God may want some from your generation to go and stay near, long enough and near enough to share deeply in the lives of those you are called to serve.

The Great Commission cannot be squeezed into a safe or comfortable mold. Jesus is on the front lines. He may be calling some of you to join him in communities at war, to bind up wounds and comfort those who mourn. Having witnessed a flesh and blood battlefield for fifteen years, it seems such places are sadly neglected by Christians.[11]

I received the following in a newsletter from Dave and Lisa, who have been faithfully working in an obscure, difficult setting in Southeast Asia for the past fourteen years, where they've made a phenomenal contribution to God's kingdom purposes. Who they are and what they have done is truly extraordinary. They've been in war zones. They've seen the miraculous. These are apostolic, pioneering types who genuinely get their thrills by going where most people would not dare to venture. In the newsletter, two paragraphs stood out as a stellar description of what an apostolic calling may entail.

When we arrived in this country, it was a good time and place for pioneering-type people. Our personality, skills and gifting are very useful when things are broken down and not yet built. We are the 'MacGyver' types who live with a Leatherman

Multi-Tool on our belt, a roll of wire, duct tape and a Maglite close at hand for when things break or go bad.

We travel with our two favorite books in double layer Ziploc bags; a *Thinline Bible* and a field medical manual. We don't need traffic laws, and can drive anything from bicycles to tractors and have fun. Beds are fine, hammocks are better (no bedbugs) and all we need is enough water to scrub the crud off once a day. We like good food, but are fine eating *other* interesting stuff. Life is good in the ambiguity zone.

These are among the committed few who have submitted themselves to an apostolic calling and consequently have aligned themselves vocationally with an apostolic structure. Through such pioneering visionaries, the good news of Jesus moves among the nations. May their tribe increase!

7

Finding Second Decision People

How to engage and release apostolic leaders

In an age of value-added through imagination, creativity and intellectual capital . . . the leader's Job One is the recruitment, development and retention of awesome talent.

Tom Peters, *Re-Imagine's Requisites: The Leadership 11*

The leaders of Great Groups love talent and know where to find it. . . . They revel in the talent of others.

Warren Bennis and Patricia Biederman, *Organizing Genius*

If you can spare them, we don't want them. If you can spare them, chances are we can spare them too.

Ronnie Stevens

The selection of leaders, and particularly those who will live and work in apostolic, second decision contexts, is a critical factor for the health and vitality of the Christian movement. J. Robert and

Richard Clinton catalog what they call "The Seven Major Leadership Lessons from the Bible." One of those lessons is that "Effective leaders view leadership selection and development as a priority function in their ministry."[1] That may seem self-evident, but it's not the way most of us live and operate. It's a principle sadly neglected in many ministry contexts.

In the West, we live in an extremely individualistic and egalitarian society. To embrace a principle like selectivity goes across the grain of much of what we value, because selectivity means that choices must be made. Value must be placed on relationships. And when choices about people are made, the choices may not seem fair.

Too often we depend on our educational institutions to do the heavy lifting when it comes to leadership selection and preparation. Ralph Winter's observation is tragically too true:

> The most extensive, pervasive strategic error in the Christian tradition lies squarely in our coveted and generously supported, but unquestioned, concept of years of "schooling" as the way for leaders to develop and be trained. . . . In this country and abroad every church movement which has come to depend solely upon residential school products for its ministry is dying.[2]

Notice the word "solely" in Winter's comment. Formal education definitely has a place and can make an enormous contribution in the life of a leader. I am the product of a couple of graduate degrees and am deeply grateful for my formal education. But there are limitations to what formal education can do. Selecting leaders on the basis of the formal educational level they have attained, or through a formal educational process, can be a serious mistake.

WHAT TO LOOK FOR

So what do I look for in identifying, challenging and developing second decision people? There are various criteria that I find useful. For example, I'm looking for those who show evidence of J. Robert Clinton's "Seven Major Leadership Lessons from the Bible"[3] in their lives. They may express these qualities intuitively, but to some extent and in some combination, they are evident.

Clinton's Seven Major Leadership Lessons

1. View present ministry in terms of a lifetime perspective.
2. Maintain a learning posture throughout life.
3. Value spiritual authority as a primary power base.
4. Demonstrate a dynamic ministry philosophy over a lifetime.
5. View leadership selection and development as a priority function in their ministry.
6. See relational empowerment as both a means and a goal of ministry.
7. Evidence a growing awareness of one's sense of destiny.

Warren Bennis, a respected author on the subject of leadership and founder of The Leadership Institute at the University of Southern California, writes about the crisis of leadership in our institutions and governments. He writes that "in many ways it is the most urgent and dangerous of the threats we face today, if only because it is insufficiently recognized and little understood."[4]

Drawing on forty years of studying leadership, Bennis says that effective leaders share five characteristics. His list is helpful and instructive in identifying apostolic leaders, and I use it as a template to find and qualify second decision people. They are individuals with the following traits:

1. They have a strong sense of purpose, a passion, a conviction, a sense of wanting to do something important to make a difference.

2. They are capable of developing and sustaining deep and trusting relationships. They seem to be constant, caring, and authentic with other people.

3. They are purveyors of hope and have positive illusions about reality.

4. They have a balance in their lives between work, power, and family or outside activities. They do not tie up all of their self-esteem in their position.

5. They have a bias toward action and, while not reckless, they do not resist taking risks.[5]

I have developed my own list over the years to describe what I look for when it comes to leadership development and training for second decision people.

• Faithfulness—I look for people who are reliable and can be trusted (2 Timothy 2:2).

• Availability—I cannot pursue someone who doesn't want to be pursued. I'm looking for eager people. Here is a true axiom: Do not give your life to the halfhearted and do not invest in those you have to constantly motivate.

• Teachability—It is not my desire to force a blessing on anyone (2 Timothy 2:2).

• Giftedness—I cannot make someone into something when God has not provided the raw material. I must be able to discern and accurately identify spiritual giftedness, acquired skills and natural abilities.

• Chemistry—If I'm going deep with a person, I need to like them and want to spend time with them (John 1:39).

• Character—A core commitment to personal integrity is an essential. When push comes to shove, will they do the right thing?

- Passion—I'm looking for people who burn with zeal for God and for the things of God. They are spiritually driven in a healthy, visionary way.

- Emotionally healthy—How great is their need for affirmation and validation? Are their emotional needs such that they will suck me and others dry looking for approval, which in reality only God can give?

- Spiritual vitality—Can they hear from God? If so, are they responsive to the Spirit and the Word and going ever deeper in dependence upon Jesus? Is there evidence that their rough edges are being refined in the process of submission to God's sanctifying rule?

THE ART OF SANCTIFIED SELECTIVITY

In the final analysis, these choices are not mine. Before he chose his twelve disciples, Jesus spent the whole night in prayer with the Father (Luke 6:12-16). He modeled not only the critical nature of such decisions but also God's sovereign prerogative to ultimately determine the outcomes.

The temptation for many in the selection of leadership and particularly second decision people is to falsely believe that the greatest leaders are those who win the most followers. Unfortunately, that can be misleading criteria. In Lindley Baldwin's words, "Such leaders are often dangerous. . . . They tend to become mob leaders, demagogues, and dictators. The greatest leadership is that which creates other leaders"—and does so from the posture of a servant.[6]

Some of my greatest mistakes in ministry have been when I have failed, for one reason or another, to embrace this principle of selectivity in leadership development.

This principle of selectivity and concentration is engraved in the universe, and will bring results no matter who practices it, whether or not the church believes it. . . . Some might object to this principle when practiced on the ground by the Christian worker that favoritism is shown toward a select group in the church. But be that as it may, it is still the way that Jesus *concentrated* His life, and it is necessary if any lasting leadership is to be trained.[7]

In the West, where we believe "all men (and women) are created equal," it can be difficult to make choices about people, as Jesus so clearly did, without appearing discriminatory or prejudiced. To the uninformed outsider, it can appear that people are written off when selectivity is exercised. I've personally been accused of this more than once, and I have the scars to prove it. Usually when the reaction was negative it wasn't because the choice was wrong but because the process was not handled well, or I had not communicated with the necessary sensitivity.

Unless it is carefully done, exercising selectivity can result in relational fallout. It's interesting that there is no evidence of such tension between the Twelve and the Seventy whom Jesus chose. Perhaps tension did occur, or perhaps Jesus was so relationally careful that no one reacted negatively. We don't know from the biblical record. But we do know that there was squabbling and jostling for position among the Twelve (Mark 10:35-45).

Selection can be more difficult for some leaders than others, depending on their gifts and the extent of their vision. Selectivity is particularly difficult for those with the gift of mercy (which would exclude me). However, the fact is that sanctified selectivity enables me to physically manage relationships and not be spread too thin. When I'm selective, going deep with a few becomes possible, so that the life change can be more profound. It is similar to what J. Robert Clinton calls his Informal Theorem: "The more informal the training medium, the more potential for in-depth impact in the life of the trainee."[8]

Exercising sanctified selectivity is an acknowledgment that not everyone has the gifts and calling to be the object of such intense leadership training and individualized development. Selectivity is a practical result of recognizing that God is uniquely at work at different places and stages with each individual. And if we do it right, selectivity is a means to a greater end. It's not elitism. Rather, it is essential for the sustainability of any movement.

DISQUALIFIERS

Let's approach this from a different perspective. What are the things that distinguish *ineffective* spiritual leaders? What do I want to look out for? What should give me pause and reason for caution? What are the disqualifiers that can indicate someone is not cut out for an apostolic ministry assignment or a second decision vocation? These are people who:

- Have issues with authority. They have never learned to be a follower.

- Experience little closure. They don't or can't complete processes, and show a lack of faithfulness in the small things (Luke 16:10-12).

- Gravitate to extremes. For example, they either tend to super-spiritualize, or they go to the opposite extreme and only understand the human dynamics of ministry, leaving little room for the supernatural.

- Have never thought through or clearly articulated their philosophy of ministry.

- Cannot tell the difference between their ambitions and God's desires, most often because they have never learned to hear from God. Their theology of guidance is underdeveloped or warped.

- Do not listen well, or don't know how to ask questions.

- Are not teachable, or exhibit an arrogant, know-it all, self-absorbed perspective.

- Evidence a critical spirit with a constant drip of paralyzing correctives.

- Cannot delegate.

- Are uniquely susceptible to acts of the flesh because they have emotional scars that haven't been adequately addressed and healed.

- Do not know themselves, nor are they in accountable, authentic or transparent relationships where self-knowledge could be acquired.

- Are overly cautious and risk averse.

THE MUCKERS

The great inventor Thomas Edison was an interesting case study in selectivity. Edison recruited a group around him he called his "Muckers." These were people with immense talent whom he recruited from all over the world, and they demonstrated curiosity, sharp reasoning, optimism and flexibility. Most of all, they wanted to work with Edison. He was a magnet for such talent, and he trusted them with his vision and his dreams.

Working with Edison was incredibly motivating. He related to the Muckers as "one of the boys," but he was also unquestionably the boss. He maintained a work environment that was classically entrepreneurial, freewheeling and informal. He brought together great people in a culture of enterprise and innovation—what he called his "invention factory"—where failure was part of the inventive process. Edison reportedly said, "The Muckers did not work to any rules or regulations because they were trying to achieve something."[9]

It is tragic when strong entrepreneurial individuals with apostolic gifting—similar to Edison's Muckers—come to the surface, and leaders don't know what to do with them. The temptation can be to use such people rather than to develop them. In my experience, there are multiple ways to frustrate, stifle and squash those with a sense of apostolic calling. If we do that, we'll never get the results Edison did.

How to Neuter Entrepreneurial, Apostolic Leaders

1. Force them to go to school.
2. Give them too much money.
3. Tell them all the reasons why something cannot be done.
4. Swamp them with paperwork and administration.
5. Give them people to lead who are excessively needy.
6. Limit their travel and keep them in their own culture.
7. Consistently correct them when they are provocative or prophetic in their communication.
8. Make sure any initiative they take must go through multiple steps of approval.
9. Insert "conserve" and "maintain" in conversations with them.
10. Have someone supervise them who projects his or her own strong pastoral gifting onto the relationship.
11. Tell them to stay when they want to go.
12. Make sure they have plenty of rules and policies to live by.
13. Give them a precise, detailed, inflexible job description.
14. Keep them safe.

SELECTIVITY AND YOUNGER LEADERS

Younger leaders in the West, particularly those with a keen sense of social justice, a desire for biblical holism and a commitment to life and ministry within community, often face unique obstacles when they are challenged to consider second decision commitments—especially in apostolic structures. It is tragic to see spiritual fervor stifled when it could be channeled for extraordinary impact. I believe we can straightjacket younger apostolic leaders when we:

1. Convince them that the need for second decision workers and ministries is passé, doesn't exist or is out of date and irrelevant in the contemporary world of postmodernity.

2. Are so passionate about social justice and a holistic gospel that we become myopic and fail to embrace the clear commands in Scripture regarding the evangelistic mandate (without which the gospel is not holistic).

3. Fail to appreciate the doctrine of spiritual gifts, and are unable or unwilling to help identify those emerging leaders gifted and called to ministry across social, linguistic or cultural barriers.

4. Persuade them that just because they are enjoying a missional life in the context of close community, they can duplicate the same form of community in another setting crossculturally or internationally.

5. Feed them the theologically and historically naive concept that the church in its modalic, local expression is all that is needed.

6. Encourage them to bury their heads in the sand and ignore the past two hundred years of missionary activity and missiological understanding. Write it all off as modern, institutional or nonorganic.

7. Help them apply missiological eyes to their *own* cultural setting, but simultaneously fail to help them apply the same understanding internationally and crossculturally.

8. Embrace a theological posture that says only "presence" is necessary for kingdom influence, as opposed to passionately persuading those far from God to become committed disciples of Jesus.

9. Present hell as a repulsive, outmoded concept that cannot be reconciled with postmodernity, thus erasing any motivation that could stem from the biblical reality that people without Jesus risk eternity separated from God.

10. Are so concerned for the purity of the church and living counterculturally that we are rarely able to *engage* contemporary culture, and remain irrelevant on the fringes.

11. Encourage them to read, think, write and blog about being missional but don't empower them to *do* much in practice.

12. Give them the impression that God is only concerned with faithfulness, not results, and deemphasize outcomes so no one can be held accountable.

13. Create a false dichotomy between obedience and intimacy with Jesus.

14. Write off mentors from the over-fifty demographic as out of touch and irrelevant.

15. Inculcate such an anti-institutional bias and suspicion of authority that they become useless in a neo-monastic or apostolic ministry that requires commitment, discipline and sacrifice.

PRINCIPLES OF SELECTION

Discussing the hard reality of selection, J. Robert Clinton describes recruiting leaders as "the deliberate effort to challenge potential leaders and to engage them in ongoing ministry so that they will develop as leaders and move toward the accomplishment of God's destiny for their lives."[10]

Over the years, I've combined some of Clinton's principles with my own experiences regarding selectivity. While I regularly apply these specifically for second decision people serving in apostolic structures, the principles have broader applicability for choosing and developing leaders in local church settings as well.

First, leaders must be deliberate and proactive in selecting emerging leaders. There must be intentionality. I approach this with great expectation that God will bring potential leaders across my path whom I can sponsor, encourage, mentor and train. They are there. My role is to find them prayerfully.

As I look for these emerging leaders, I must do it in the most appropriate ways possible. My purpose is to enlist them in the willful pursuit of God's design for their lives. This will require discernment and sensitivity to the uniqueness of different people, and to the notion that different people will require different means to be selected and motivated, particularly when a second decision commitment is involved. Astute leaders help people to recognize their calling using different methods to motivate them, depending on who they are, what they want out of life and what they value. This means we must woo second decision people to our causes with different means, depending on the person. It's very situational. We need to assess where they are and use what uniquely fits them in order to attract their attention and to challenge them onward to God's best for their lives.[11]

Good leaders challenge people to a larger, more satisfying existence and life purpose. This is a powerful incentive in the motivation of second decision leaders. Potential leaders tend to live up to the genuine expectations of older leaders they admire. Seeing beyond where someone *is* to what they *can become* is a powerful motivational technique, but it must be carefully exercised with integrity. Seeing the best in someone and believing that they will fulfill their potential is the first step in moving them in that direction. This formidable relational dynamic assumes some important prerequisites:

- Emerging leaders and older leaders are in relationships of meaning.

- Older leaders understand such a principle and see the value in it. They are willing to invest in such relationships.

- Those with grey hair have also earned the respect of the newcomers and are models worth emulating.

- The emerging leaders are teachable and want to learn from those who have gone before.

- The older leaders know how to mentor, coach and communicate expectations with a genuineness, humility and transparency that inspires.

Jesus recruited *from the fringes*, not from the current religious leadership establishment, which had very fixed paradigms. He was looking for people who could be shaped, people who were not already "in the box." Therefore, I try to "swing for the fences" when I challenge second decision people about their life choices. I want to project their vision into places where they would not normally imagine themselves, and then gradually reel back to a place where they can be visionary, yet realistic. This means visualizing the best people in the most difficult places, and then seeing what is palatable. I challenge people with Dawson Trotman's admonition: "Never do anything others can do or will do, when there are things to be done that others can't do or won't."[12]

I consistently find that my best environment for identifying and selecting second decision people is real life experience, where I can do things together with someone. Jesus trained the Twelve in the midst of his ministry to the multitudes. *More is caught than is taught.* This means intentionally providing opportunities where younger leaders can cominister alongside more mature, experienced leaders. This model raises the status of emerging leaders toward the status of the established leaders with whom they are working, gives them broad exposure to the organization's people and provides experiential learning.

I try to never go anywhere alone. I always want someone with me—otherwise it is a wasted opportunity. One of the best ways I have of sharing my experience and life with younger leaders is to get them to travel with me and immerse themselves in ministry settings around the world. It's amazing what can be accomplished through many hours together on an airplane, punctuated by on-the-ground experiences with people in the trenches of real life and ministry, especially those in challenging crosscultural venues.

I have learned to follow social networks to find people called to second decision ministry. This works because second decision people often know other people of similar heart and commitment. Each person helps identify the next person in the network, since they are naturally attracted to one another. Jesus used a similar method when he found some of his first disciples among John the Baptist's disciples. It's like mining a vein of gold.

I've also found that the community (or the team) recruits best. I always want to introduce prospective people to already-committed people, who are models of what that person could be and experience. I want the person exposed to others who are passionate, winsome and contagious.

Jesus demonstrated a balanced and holistic gospel which was attractive to those he challenged to second decision commitment. He especially used spiritual power and the supernatural as part of his technique, which was a demonstration and confirmation of his spiritual authority. Authenticity is a result of such spiritual authority and a magnet for others looking for ways to make their lives count.

In the final analysis, leadership selection is the key to an ongoing effective ministry that can span generations. It is ultimately a divine process—it is God who chooses. Jesus spent the whole night in prayer with the Father before setting aside the Twelve (Luke 6:12). Robert Coleman lays it out clearly when he says:

> [Jesus'] concern was not with programs to reach the multitudes, but with men whom the multitudes would follow. . . . Men were to be his method of winning the world to God. . . .

The world is desperately seeking someone to follow. This is the decisive question of our age. The relevance of all that we do waits on its verdict, and in turn, the destiny of multitudes hangs in the balance.[13]

When my mortal existence is over and done, I want nothing more than a legacy that has emulated the life of Jesus in the way he imparted vision and life to a handful of his closest followers. I am convinced beyond all doubt that such an investment in the lives of carefully selected second decision leaders, who can in turn multiply in succeeding generations, will affect the course of history and alter the fate of nations for the sake of the name of Jesus.

How happy are those
who take the Gospel
to other lands.
They obey your command
Lord Jesus
Your command to tell
the Good News
everywhere
to every person
in the whole world.
They forsake
kindred and friends
houses and land
comfort security things
to go tell
teach
heal
love.
They are the great ones
of this generation

of whom the world
is not worthy.
They are the ones whom
the world pities.
Poor world
Poor pitiful world
They are Your ambassadors
sent by you
to declare an end to hostility
and announce peace
through Your death
and endless life.
How happy are those
who take the Gospel
To other lands.[14]

—Joseph Bayly

Running Together!

The exponential leverage of interdependence

In the Scriptures one discovers congregations along with specialized ministries for extending the church and strengthening all congregations. The itinerant apostolic missionary teams would be one example of such a ministry that was not bound to a congregation. . . .

The church's nature as both one and catholic means that these structures must exist in a symbiotic relationship with local congregations and their denominational structures.

Darrell Guder, *Missional Church*

An unchurchly mission is as much a monstrosity as an unmissionary church.

Lesslie Newbigin, *The Household of God*

For many years Leadership Network has provided a significant service to the church in North America by facilitating dialogue between leaders of different ministries. In 1995, I was fortunate enough to be included in one such three-day gathering where a dozen leaders from missionary organizations met with the pastors responsible for the mission efforts of a dozen prominent mega-churches. The idea was to sequester us in the room for three days, let us set the agenda and talk.

As we gathered the first evening to get acquainted over dinner, I was seated at a round table with eight others when one of the pastors directly across from me spied my nametag. "Are you the guy who wrote that recent article in *Evangelical Missions Quarterly*?" he asked. "Yes, that's me," I said. The article was entitled "When Local Churches Act Like Agencies" and was an apologetic for the legitimacy and independence of apostolic mission entities.[1]

The pastor looked squarely at me and declared—in a voice that everyone else at the table could hear—"I wondered who the ass was who wrote that article!" Ouch! Needless to say, this was the beginning of several stimulating days of conversation. The irony is that twenty years later, that same pastor ended up joining CRM and making the jump from a local church to an apostolic, missionary structure.

I tell that story simply to illustrate the fact that the tension between the church in its apostolic, missionary form and the church in its local, congregational form can be very real. When we don't understand how these two God-designed expressions of the body of Christ can and should work interdependently, it takes an unnecessary toll on our effectiveness and undermines our ability to serve a watching world.

TWO LEGS AND ONE PAIR OF PANTS

Throughout church history, I think it's clear that when modalities and sodalities have worked interdependently and cooperatively, with appropriate freedom and a clear understanding of the roles and strengths of each, there have been great advances in the progress of the gospel. The blessing of God has been manifest. So what is needed is cooperation and partnership.

I see both modalities and sodalities as part of God's total plan for the church in mission. However, if the mission is to be fulfilled, the two must relate to each other in a dynamic way. Both should be considered structures that bind together the people of God. They are kingdom structures, and they exist for God's glory. Both in the true sense of the word are part of the *church.*

The main point is that in order to accomplish the mission of the church, sodalities and modalities need each other in a symbiotic relationship. The symbiotic relationship means that each one contributes to the well being of the other.[2]

So how does interdependence work out in practice? What happens?

There will be tension. It comes with the turf. What each of these structures emphasizes touches on the inherent weakness of the other. Consequently, each must speak prophetically to the other, and there will be clashes of values. It is as predictable as the sun coming up tomorrow morning. It is not a character problem on the part of either, nor is it a lack of spirituality.

For example, take local church leaders' strength in caring for people. I know some local churches that are disturbed by how apostolic people can be chewed up when they work for a missionary entity, particularly in crosscultural ministry assignments. Churches want to know why this happens. Who's caring for these people? Are we shooting our wounded? It's particularly worrisome to them if the wounded people were originally from their own congregation.

I met with one pastor who was concerned about an incident involving people working for our organization who were supported by his congregation. We had deployed this family as part of a team outside of North America, and a significant moral problem had come up. It was hidden, unforeseen and unpredictable.

I tried to assure him that we were not cavalier about what had happened and had invested an enormous amount of supervisory time in the situation. Our Staff Development and Care Team—made up of counselors, therapists, spiritual directors and trainers—had been actively involved. But he still wondered if we were doing enough. In the end, the marriage of the people in question disintegrated and with much regret we let the couple go—something an apostolic structure can and sometimes must do. Ultimately, what was playing out was a values clash between the two redemptive structures. Neither was wrong. Just different.

The strengths of each need to be accessible to the other. I've seen the benefits to a local congregation when their people are trained in evangelism by Cru, or when Richard Foster can be their mentor in spiritual formation and spiritual disciplines, or when their people are exposed to the financial philosophy and tools of Crown Ministries. There is an inestimable contribution made to local churches when their people sponsor children through World Vision or Compassion, study the Bible in depth through Bible Study Fellowship, and see the younger generation in their communities reached through Young Life or internationally with YWAM. The smorgasbord of possibilities is phenomenal and should never be threatening.

Certainly, the larger the church the greater the possibility that it can design such specialized ministry on its own. But smaller churches with fewer resources can benefit hugely through the use of such "plug-and-play" resources. As of 2015, 60 percent of the Protestant churches in the United States have one hundred or fewer adults on a typical weekend, and just two percent of churches attract more than one thousand adults per weekend.[3] So the percentage of churches that have the scale or resources for such specialization is very small.

Likewise, the resources of a local congregation can be an enormous blessing to those who have become "sent ones." The prayer covering.

The financial support. The pastoral concern and care. The human resources. Everything that local churches are uniquely equipped to offer can be an incredible gift to those serving in sodalities, and through them to a hurting world.

When our daughter, Christine, was two years old we were on a family vacation, camping in a state park near Birmingham, Alabama. By mistake I fed her some cashews, not realizing that her severe peanut allergy could also mean that cashews were toxic and potentially fatal. We nearly lost her. The experience was harrowing. When she was finally stabilized in a children's hospital in Birmingham, we received two phone calls almost immediately: one was from our home church in Southern California and the other from the pastor of one of our major supporting churches in the Birmingham area. They were right there. Spot on. Ready and able to care, extend compassion, meet our needs and provide the type of support we desperately needed in the midst of a serious crisis.

Does that mean sodalities can't or won't provide such care? No. But modalities are so much better at it. It's part of their DNA, and they have more of the right resources to make it work. It is a wonderful contribution that they bring to the relationship.

Harvesting and conserving. When these two structures work synergistically, the Christian movement thrives with health and vitality. Let's use an agricultural analogy. Grain needs to be picked and it needs to be conserved. Both are essential. It does a farmer no good to expand his fields and plant more crops if he can't handle the harvest when it comes in.

Although difficult to measure, it is estimated that the postharvest loss of food in the developing world can be as high as 65 percent.[4] The waste is crippling when what is harvested cannot be adequately stored, processed and distributed. It's the same in the Christian movement: both harvesting and conserving are crucial.

This is exactly what happened when Celtic apostolic bands

moved into new areas and pioneered new ground. Wherever they went, scores of local parishes sprung up around them. These parishes conserved the fruit the apostolic bands generated. They did not compete with them. Together, the missionaries and the parish churches laid a solid foundation for the Christian movement in Ireland, Scotland, England and parts of Europe that lasted for over a thousand years.

Part of the genius of the Celtic movement was that the two structures worked together. Certainly the relationship had its tensions, but what resulted from their cooperation was a missional synergy that produced a version of the Christian movement that was extraordinarily viral.

Partnership increases scope and effectiveness. InterVarsity excels at ministering among university students and faculty. Young Life is one of the best in the world at ministry to younger students. Does that mean a local congregation should not reach out and minister to local college students or that they should not have a youth ministry? Of course not. But cooperating with these specialized agencies provides expertise, understanding and a missional dynamic that the local church on its own could rarely realize.

Does this mean a local congregation has no responsibility to get involved when a disaster occurs somewhere around the world—a tsunami in Southeast Asia, an earthquake in Haiti or a famine in East Africa? Absolutely not. But the ideal scenario is when the local congregation can partner with those who excel in crisis environments. The optimal response is for local churches to operate hand-in-hand with those specialized forms of the church that are specifically called and equipped for such situations. Specialists fill a niche that generalists cannot.

After the Berlin Wall came down and communism began to disintegrate across Eastern Europe, CRM had teams launching into formerly communist countries—people who knew the language, were culturally capable and were committed to living incarnationally in these difficult contexts. In those turbulent days there was a surge of compassion and interest from the West toward Eastern Europe—a region once militantly closed to the Christian movement and now open. Resources poured in from churches and individuals who were deeply moved to help. But the waste was considerable. There was little thought given to what effective ministry ought to look like in such a challenging crosscultural environment. Well-meaning people made many mistakes regarding where they gave money and what relationships they trusted. The uninformed investment of money from the Western world became a negative and corrupting influence.

However, there were some savvy local churches in the West that understood the pitfalls and appreciated the value of partnership. As they partnered with our teams and other missionaries on the ground in Eastern Europe and the former Soviet Union, the results were remarkable. As money and resources were moved into those areas, these churches depended on our people on site to qualify the recipients, monitor the progress and ensure that the results were reported with integrity. Working together produced exemplary results.

CAN MEGACHURCHES DO IT ALL?

A go-it-alone attitude is common among megachurches who feel they don't need outside apostolic structures. That is understandable in congregations that are one-stop shops, and tend to be closed systems. And because they have been successful (after a fashion), there is a genuine conviction that they can do what separate apostolic structures do, and do it better. Who needs outside entities?

The truth is that sometimes megachurches can perform apostolic functions well. That's especially true if they are willing to give a significant degree of internal freedom and autonomy to their own apostolic, missionary initiatives. This may mean that the mega-church actually creates its own sodalities—outside and alongside the megachurch—to focus on a specific missional task. These structures can give apostolic leaders within the church an outlet for their gifts and passion. It's an example of a modality spawning a sodality: a healthy way for sodalities to be created.

In the United States, there are around sixteen hundred Protestant churches that fit the definition of a megachurch (a local church with over two thousand adult participants).[5] In many ways, it is helpful to think of a megachurch as a denominational structure in one location, a kind of unilocational denomination. It makes sense that some of these would create their own apostolic structures to send their people across cultural, linguistic, social and geographic barriers.

However, there can be a downside when amateurs get involved in a game that requires professional expertise. For example, a local church or even a megachurch could never do the Bible translation work that Wycliffe Bible Translators is so skilled at doing. Or consider the expertise of the International Justice Mission in advocating for women trapped in the sex trade. Even the most committed local church could never duplicate the quality or sophistication of these ministries. As Alan Hirsch reminds us:

> The greatest silencing of the call for change often comes from leaders of large churches. They seem to be unaware of or untouched by any effects of significant social change. We have both been told more than once by large-church pastors that the church isn't doing so badly at all. This false sense of security is chicken-run thinking, where the shackles are primarily in the minds and consciousness of the inmates.[6]

However, the vast majority of Christians, both in North America and worldwide, are not in megachurches. Approximately 80 percent of the churches in North America have less than two hundred people, and 60 percent less than one hundred. The incentive for these churches to partner with sodalities should be all the greater.

BEING GENEROUS

The jury is still out as to whether consistent, sacrificial giving will be as strong in emerging generations as it has been for the baby boomers. But even if giving remains consistent among churchgoers, the sheer decline in numbers of committed followers of Jesus in the United States—if the trends continue—will have a huge effect on the financial resources available for ministry. In the next three decades, overall giving to churches could drop by as much as 70 percent in North America.[7]

This dwindling of available resources is symptomatic of the continuing decline of Christianity in North America and in the West in general,[8] and it reflects a deeper, more fundamental problem: an underlying lack of spiritual health and vitality. Hirsch and Catchim tell us that the church in the United States spends over $70 billion every decade on church plants and resources, but that even so "we are experiencing decline in adherence and membership at an unprecedented rate."[9]

I was once invited to a meeting with the leaders of a local church in southern California who had concerns about the number of people who had left their fellowship to serve with our organization around the world. It was a church of around three to four hundred people, so this exodus into apostolic ministry was quite visible. A senior high pastor, junior high pastor, adult singles leader and two people from the church's elder board had left to serve as missionaries with us.

As the meeting began things were a bit tense. Were we "plundering" their congregation and "sheep stealing"? My answer to them was twofold. First, we were providing opportunities for their people to live out their calling for the world. We were not competing with them, but were part of the same team—carrying out a separate and necessary function as part of the larger body of Christ. Then I turned to Proverbs 11:24-25. "Let's substitute the word *church* for the word *man* in this passage," I suggested. "One church gives freely, yet gains even more; another withholds unduly, but comes to poverty. A generous church will prosper; whoever refreshes others will be refreshed."

My encouragement to them was, "If we work together, this can be a win-win for everyone." While I'm not sure I was 100 percent persuasive, at least we got on the same page in discussing what our partnership could look like with a larger kingdom perspective.[10]

RESPONSIBLE APOSTOLICITY

I've done it. In my frustration with local churches and pastoral leaders, I have occasionally wanted to bypass them, refusing to believe they will ever change. To be honest, it's an all-too-common attitude for those of us in the world of missions when we run up against the attitudes and inertia in some local churches.

A national leader serving with us in the Middle East tells the story of his frustrating involvement in a local congregation. The political infighting, traditionalism, lack of missionality and legalism was overwhelmingly discouraging. Finally, in disgust, he told the church leadership, "Jesus didn't die for this!" and walked away (for a time) from that particular local church.

I understand the frustration. I've been in some of those environments in that part of the world, and they can be stifling. But at the same time, these remain legitimate expressions of the body of Christ. While I suspect that Jesus, the Lord of the church, is anguished over what is done in his name, these people still belong to him. And what breaks his heart should break ours also. So whenever possible, I partner. I do all I can to cooperate.

Of course the question could be asked: When does a local church cease to be a legitimate expression of what genuine Christianity is all about? When should we wipe the dust from our feet and move on (Luke 10:11), and give up on the possibility of partnership?

During one period of living and working out of London, I was walking in the West End and came across a massive and imposing church building—not a rare experience in a city where steeples can be seen just about any direction you look. The Christian legacy of a bygone era prevails in London's architecture, if not in the hearts and minds of those living in its thoroughly post-Christian culture. I found an open door and went in. The interior of the church was spectacular: exquisite stained glass, a huge vaulted ceiling, and stone and woodwork that were remarkable in their artistry.

It was just me and a woman doing some cleaning. We talked. She told me there are about one hundred and thirty active members of this congregation, in a building that could easily accommodate a thousand or more. It was a church that was struggling to minister to its dwindling congregation. Incredibly depressing! As I marveled at this beautiful architectural relic, the words that came were almost audible: "Jesus has left the building!"

From there, I wandered across the street and came across a completely different scene. It was a Saturday morning, open-air swap meet, swarming with hundreds of people from every imaginable ethnic background. The smells, colors and languages all made for a wonderfully diverse and vibrant setting. Interestingly, I sensed that Jesus was in the midst of that crowd, longing for followers—and that's where he wanted me to join him.

Tragically, there may be times when "Jesus has left the building" and his presence and anointing have been lifted from a group of people who claim allegiance to him in name only. It can happen in a megachurch, a house group, a denominational gathering, a church in the jungle of Papua New Guinea or a cathedral in Europe.

Scattered throughout our organization around the world are

some wonderful people who have the spiritual gift of the discerning of spirits, which means they can see, to one degree or another, into the supernatural realm. I don't have this gift, even though Jesus and I have had some extended conversations about it. But it is an incredible encouragement to know and trust those who have been given this gift, and who know how to exercise it with maturity and discernment, and not with sensationalism.

One of these folks related to me her experience in London the first time she visited St. Paul's Cathedral, the massive Anglican cathedral in the heart of the city. She was stunned to see—in the supernatural realm—angels moving up and down the aisles, longing for worship that *was not happening*. Talk about Jesus having left the building.

So what do we do with all this? How do those of us in apostolic sodalities know when to fish and when to cut bait in our pursuit of interdependence and authentic partnership? I believe that's something that only God can make clear. On the one hand, part of our calling as apostolic people is to do all we can to be conduits of renewal, life, vision and spiritual vigor to our brothers and sisters in local churches—no matter what their history or the particular models they embrace. This has been the historical pattern throughout church history, and it must be pursued with great humility and grace. It's all too easy for apostolic people to assume the air of the spiritual expert, or an attitude of one-upmanship. But that serves no purpose and is hurtful for all involved.

On the other hand, God may not be at work in some of these religious environments, from which genuine spiritual life and vitality have departed. As a result, it may be time to "go into the highways and the byways" and bypass the religious establishment (Matthew 22 and Luke 14).

Thus our commitment has remained a "both/and." In our ministry at CRM, we've struggled for many years to find a balance between focusing our efforts on and through *what is* versus working directly with what *could be* among the unreached, unchurched and dechurched. It's an ongoing tension that we embrace and are willing to live with. We do so because we believe Jesus hasn't given up on what is. But simultaneously, we believe it is impossible for "what is" to fulfill the mission of God on their own.

SHED THE ENTITLEMENT

I must confess it's not unusual for apostolic people ministering in sodalities to slip into an arrogant attitude, believing that they are entitled to the resources—both human and financial—that can be provided by the local church. Sometimes we drool with envy when we imagine what *we* could do with all those resources. The temptation is always there to hijack the local church's resources and reinvest them in ways we believe would produce greater kingdom results.

As a general rule, modalities have greater access to resources than sodalities. I know that may seem like an unfair generalization, particularly when economic times are tough and in some contexts local churches do struggle financially. But by comparison, apostolic structures have historically tended to be leaner and more starved for resources. They rarely have the same breadth of constituents to draw from as local congregations.

There is an office in London that's part of the Anglican Church called the Division of Redundant Churches. Essentially, it's a real estate office. It exists to sell off church property that is no longer sustainable. They work to unload property that the Church of England can no longer afford. Presently, there are sixteen thousand Anglican Church buildings in the UK, and from 1969 to 2010, 1,795 church buildings were closed—11 percent of the building stock.[11] Interestingly, the number of mosques that have opened in Britain during the same time period has almost been equal to the Church of England closures—1,689.[12] Meanwhile, the Methodist church in

Great Britain is closing approximately one hundred church buildings per year.[13]

At the same time, there are vibrant and vital ministries in London that struggle greatly with a lack of resources—particularly housing. The frustration of seeing so many resources languishing and simultaneously so many resources desperately needed in the same context can be overwhelming to those who are serious about the mission of God in a world-class city like London. But it's not unusual. The misappropriation of resources can be seen in almost every major urban center in the post-Christian West.

When there are tensions over resources, it is immensely helpful for everyone involved to realize that none of it belongs to any of us anyway. We are all simply stewards of the kingdom resources that that have been entrusted to us. Maintaining a kingdom perspective can be an effective antidote to entitlement. We need to remind ourselves that the King of the kingdom is not limited by a lack of resources. He owns it all, and he will distribute it to accomplish his purposes.

THE JOY OF WORKING TOGETHER

When there is healthy synergy between modalities and sodalities the results can be remarkable. And movements of the gospel will not happen unless these essential parts of the body of Christ work together. It's like an engine with several essential parts that must work together for the whole contraption to be effective. We need each other.

> During a lengthy period of time, perhaps a thousand years, the building and rebuilding of the modalities was mainly the work of the sodalities. That is to say the monasteries were uniformly the source and the real focal point of new energy and vitality which flowed into the diocesan side of the Christian movement. . . .
>
> At many points there was rivalry between these two struc-

tures, between bishop and abbot, diocese and monastery, modality and sodality, but the great achievement of the medieval period is the ultimate synthesis, delicately achieved, whereby Catholic orders were able to function along with Catholic parishes and dioceses without the two structures conflicting with each other to the point of a setback to the movement. The harmony between the modality and the sodality achieved by the Roman Church is perhaps the most significant characteristic of this phase of the world Christian movement and continues to be Rome's greatest organizational advantage to this day.[14]

So let's learn from the past and do this together. Partnering. Co-operating. Demonstrating the kind of relational and operational synergy that brings extraordinary results and pleases the God who calls us. He expects no less—and the world that awaits our message demands it.

9

Movements of God

The extraordinary results of apostolic gifting lived out in apostolic structures

It's great to want to be part of something, but it's a different thing completely to believe wholly in some type of movement, and to give everything for that something.

Brandon Boyd

The mission of the Celtic branch had rescued Western civilization and restored movemental Christianity in Europe.

George Hunter III, *The Celtic Way of Evangelism*

Tell the students to give up their small ambitions and come eastward to preach the gospel of Christ.

Francis Xavier

was in Iraq. The man sitting across from me had been a jihadist. About two years previously, through a series of supernatural events, the gift of a Bible and subsequent dreams and visions, he had decided wholeheartedly to follow Jesus, a decision of no little consequence in this context.

"I know how to form and multiply cells," he told me with a sly smile. He had been well trained as a jihadist and knew what it took to catalyze a movement. The lessons from his past had direct applicability to his new commitment to movements that make and multiply disciples of Jesus. "We're not interested in creating elephant churches in this place," he continued. "We want people who follow Jesus to be in groups that multiply like rabbits."

Such dedication to the creation of a movement has been repeated over and over again throughout history, with astonishing results. And as this former terrorist's story illustrates, these principles and methods have been used for evil as well as good.

CAPTURING THE DYNAMIC

Douglas Hyde had been the editor of the *Daily Worker*, the newspaper of the Communist Party of Great Britain, but in 1948 he resigned, left the party and publically converted to Christianity. Subsequently he authored a famous book, *Dedication and Leadership*, which was both an exposé and a handbook on how communism had been built into the most powerful movement of the twentieth century—a movement which at its zenith encompassed almost 50 percent of the world's population and contributed to close to one hundred million deaths.[1]

What is remarkable about Hyde's book is the extraordinary similarity between the communist methodology for creating and sustaining a movement and what has been true of the followers of Jesus for two thousand years. While the ends are radically different, the means of the two movements bear many similarities. Hyde writes that "much of the Communist success has come from forms of activity and an approach to people which might as easily, and with more justification, be used by Christians."[2]

Hyde also observes that in general, Christians have rarely embodied the dedication and leadership necessary to create and sustain a movement. Few Christians have understood what it is to be a movement, and even fewer have been willing to participate in something that will demand their all. For those who have, the results have influenced the course of history. Hyde acknowledges that one of the few places he has observed such commitment has been in the Roman Catholic orders—among those people who have taken vows and committed themselves vocationally to one another and to a life of radical missionality.

Both communism and extreme Islamic fundamentalism are evil counterfeits of the movement dynamics deeply embedded in the Christian movement from its very beginning. Jesus himself modeled these dynamics, and the book of Acts is a fascinating textbook on how his followers lived them out in the first century. The outcomes were so extraordinary that within three centuries, one of the most brutal empires in human history had been thoroughly infected and overrun by an unstoppable movement begun by an obscure Galilean carpenter.

For the past two thousand years, thousands of people have repeatedly demonstrated the validity of these dynamics and fueled submovements of the greater Christian movement. Their commitment has been so strong that their lives have sometimes been forfeited so that the name of Jesus can be honored among the nations.

One of the more thorough studies that gets to the heart of the movement Jesus started is A. B. Bruce's *The Training of the Twelve*, first published in 1871.[3] Robert Coleman's *The Master Plan of Evangelism* is a more current, concise treatment of the same topic.[4] But despite the clarity of such presentations and the compelling nature of their content, their philosophy of ministry gets little traction in the contemporary church. "When [Jesus'] plan is reflected on, the basic philosophy is so different from that of the modern church that its implications are nothing less than revolutionary."[5] That is not surprising, since the church in its local form rarely generates movements on its own. To be the sole agent generating and sustaining a movement is not part of the local church's DNA, and it is really unfair to expect it to be something God never intended.

APOSTOLIC MOVEMENTS

I confess to being nervous at times when I use the term *movement*, for fear it will become a cliché and lose its punch. I am afraid it will go the way of "missional," "discipleship," "community," "spiritual formation"—you name it—words and phrases that we've heard so often we hardly remember what they mean anymore.

Here is the general definition I use of any movement: *The sociological phenomenon that takes place when a group of people work together to passionately advance their shared commitments.*

The world has seen many kinds of movements, and not just religious ones: the movement to abolish slavery in England in the eighteenth century, the American civil rights movement, the environmental movement, the feminist movement and so on. Movements can powerfully change the world and affect the course of history, for good or ill. There is a transformational dynamic and a unique energy that accompanies a movement when it begins to impact the hearts and imaginations of the people involved.

But the movements I want to highlight have a unique dimension to them. When the Spirit of God breathes supernatural power into a movement so that the focus of the movement is the good news of Jesus and his kingdom's presence, a profound difference is made. Therefore, *apostolic movements occur when the good news of Jesus spreads contagiously—like a relational virus—through a network of social relationships whereby many people become committed followers of Jesus and groups of these disciples rapidly multiply, radically impacting whole towns, cities, and nations with the presence of his kingdom.*

RESULTS MATTER

The result of genuine missionality should be such movements. And apostolic people working through apostolic structures are a key ingredient in catalyzing, multiplying and sustaining these movements.

If we look at the entire history of the Christian movement and the myriad of submovements within in, it is hard to find examples of such movements that did not have, at their core, apostolic people functioning through apostolic structures. Apostolic people (1) are often the catalysts and prime movers at the beginning of movements, (2) are found at critical hinge points on which the ongoing momentum of a movement depends, (3) facilitate the multiplication of movements and (4) are usually foundational to being and developing movement leadership.

Whenever we see movements in the history of Christianity, there are usually three things that come together: (1) the right people, (2) the right structures and (3) the sovereign anointing of God.

Structure matters. Passion is never enough. Whenever we find movements resulting from people sold out to the mission of God and experiencing his sovereign, powerful presence, apostolic structure is always in the equation.

An insightful treatment of movement and movement dynamics is Steve Addison's book *Movements That Change the World*.[6] Steve makes the case that apostolic movements have five distinct characteristics:

1. White-hot faith

2. Commitment to a cause

3. Contagious relationships

4. Rapid mobilization

5. Adaptive methods

While I agree wholeheartedly with Steve's analysis in *Movements*

That Change the World and in his excellent subsequent volume, *What Jesus Started*,[7] I would emphasize that in each of the case studies Steve uses, the presence of apostolic people and structures was *always* an essential component and cannot be overlooked. There is always a strong structural dynamic in the generation, sustainability and ongoing momentum of a movement. While the necessary structure may be unintentional or intuitive, it is still inevitable in any sustainable gospel movement.

Even when there appears to be little *human* recognition of movement dynamics, there is always a *divine* intentionality. The challenge for effective leadership is to discern that divine orchestration—what God is doing—and then cooperate.

This is the defining difference between a George Whitfield and a John Wesley. While Whitfield was one of, if not *the* leading figure of American Christianity in his day, it was Wesley whose influence lasted for hundreds of years because of his organizational skills. Wesley understood structure and knew how to use it. Whitfield was a powerful voice for the gospel in his generation, but structure and organizational skills were not his focus. On the other hand, the Methodists were like an ever growing furnace with a fire that was constantly stoked and expanding. Whitfield was a superb communicator; Wesley a superb organizer.

MOVEMENT CHARACTERISTICS

Building on Steve Addison's insights, here is my list of movement characteristics and how each relates to apostolic structure.

Movements don't rely on voluntary members to lead and are rarely egalitarian or democratic. They have committed participants who demonstrate a high level of purpose and sacrifice with a deep devotion to God's anointed leaders.

In the early years of the Salvation Army—before it was called an "army"—the fledgling movement and its leader, William Booth, went through a significant crisis. Institutionalization, endless committees, group decision making and tedious processes had all bogged down the ministry to the point that Booth, greatly discouraged, wrote:

> The poor convert who had been brought to the penitent-form two months since must appear trembling before an elders' meeting. . . . If he ventured to aspire to public speaking, he must pass another examination before the exhorters' meeting. Did he wish to distribute tracts, then he must see the tract committee. . . . If the tract distributor came across cases of extreme need, then he must apply to another committee for the help to the extent of a shilling or two which he might be allowed to give. By-and-by would come round the solemn day for the meetings of the local preachers and the quarterly meetings. . . . Oh, those elders' meetings . . . prolonged till midnight many a time.[8]

Exasperated, Booth moved decisively to change course and radically reinvent what was quickly morphing into a stagnant modality structure, and threatening to destroy the momentum of the Salvationist movement. Booth was called to "war," and his mission demanded an apostolic structure capable of fighting and winning. It was a holy battle for the souls of men and women. No more endless meetings. No more committees. No more conferences to decide direction. No more collegial leadership. He wrote,

> We are sent to war. We are not sent to minister to a congregation and be content if we keep things going. We are sent to make war . . . and to stop short of nothing but the subjugation of the world to the sway of the Lord Jesus. We must bear that in mind in all our plans . . . our aim is to put down the kingdom of the devil. . . . This mission is going to be what its officers make it.[9]

This story illustrates some interesting dynamics of decision making among apostolic people and the movements that they generate. They are rarely collegial or consensual in their decision making. They must be nimble and able to respond quickly to needs and change. This requires people with strong leadership gifts who are given the freedom—and the trust from their followers—to make decisions without being bogged down by group discernment and egalitarian forms of structure.

I know that this assertion goes against the grain of some present-day leadership theory. There is certainly value in situational leadership, adaptive styles and relying on a diversity of giftedness and temperaments. I am not advocating a direct leadership style as the only tool in the toolbox, or suggesting that every ministry situation is a nail to be driven with that same hammer. Indeed, in some cultures the importance of the group surpasses the individual. But whatever the nuance, movement leadership is always decisive. Leaders lead. People follow. There is momentum and results.

I have had many pressures over the years, often from well-meaning people within our organization, to rely more on group discernment and participatory decision making. I have steadfastly resisted the pressure, sometimes at great relational cost, to lead using democratic processes where everyone gets a voice. Many of the pressures are cultural, unconsciously carried over from our Western assumption that the majority always makes the best decision. It doesn't always work that way in focused, task-oriented missional structures—for numerous reasons.

First, such group discernment—popular among traditions like the Brethren, the Mennonites, the Quakers and others who are congregationally oriented—can negate and neuter the spiritual gift of leadership and frustrate those with apostolic roles. In these egalitarian systems, the leader may become merely the facilitator-in-chief. Furthermore, the process can mean that an entire decision-making process can be held hostage by the loudest, the most fearful, the most contrary or the most immature person in the room. As we know from political philosophy and the abundant testimony of history, the will of the majority or a consensus does not always guarantee the right decision.

Second, local churches sometimes have the luxury of time and resources to patiently study issues and take their time during their decision-making process. But that is not the case for many right-footed people. Apostolic people and structures must jealously guard their freedom to respond nimbly to challenges. They must maintain their flexibility. Indecisiveness and an aversion to risk can be more costly than daring and decisiveness. "More failure comes from an excess of caution than from bold experiments with new ideas. The frontiers of the Kingdom of God were never advanced by men and women of caution."[10]

Movements have an agenda for change. If there is no change and vision is not being realized, then something is wrong. This means movements are not about maintenance. They are about pioneering and taking new ground. They are about transformation. When evaluating whether he was accomplishing his God-given mission, William Booth also wrote, "I should conclude I was out of my place if I spent twelve months at a place and did not leave it tangibly, unmistakably, visibly better than I found it."[11]

Movements are made up of people passionately committed to a common cause. It's the air they breathe, the reason they exist. I traveled extensively in Eastern Europe and parts of the former Soviet Union in the decade before the demise of communism. I saw firsthand the results of a once-powerful movement that had ossified into an evil, totalitarian system. The Soviet Union of the latter half of the twentieth century was a far cry from the passionate movement that John Reed described in his book *Ten Days That Shook the World*.[12] Made into the epic movie *Reds* (starring Warren Beatty and Diane

Keaton), Reed's story is a stirring account of passionate people committed to a common cause. It is a riveting example of what motivates people to give their lives to something that matters, even if that cause turns out to be false and deceptive.

"The mass of men lead lives of quiet desperation," wrote Henry David Thoreau.[13] And Oliver Wendell Holmes wrote, "Alas for those that never sing, / But die with all their music in them!"[14] Commitment to a movement is one of the strongest possible antidotes to such meaninglessness in the human condition.

Movements transcend personalities. No one person can control a movement and it is foolish to try. J. Edwin Orr has one book devoted entirely to the worldwide revival and subsequent great awakening of 1858–1859.[15] He tells how the phenomenon of an outpouring of the Spirit of God, not dissimilar to Acts 2, spontaneously emerged in South Africa in the parish of Andrew Murray. Murray, a Scottish-educated, Dutch Reformed pastor in the Cape, later gained worldwide fame because of his extensive writings (over two hundred and forty books). Orr writes:

> One Sunday evening, sixty young people were gathered in a hall . . . several had risen to announce the singing of a hymn and to offer prayer, when a Fingo girl [a South African tribe] in the employ of a farmer asked if she might do the same. Permission granted, after hesitation, the girl poured out a moving prayer . . . while she was praying, a roll of noise like that of approaching thunder was heard, coming closer and closer until it enveloped the hall, shaking the place. The company burst into prayer, a majority audibly, a minority in murmuring tones. An unusual outpouring of the Holy appeared to be taking place. Andrew Murray walked among the distressed people calling for silence, "Mense, bly stil! Mense, bly stil!" No one took the slightest notice. . . .

The outpouring continued and in a subsequent meeting, Murray took a lead by reading a passage of Scripture and giving his pastoral commentary. Then he engaged in prayer and invited others so to do. Again the mysterious roll of approaching thunder was heard in distance, coming nearer and nearer, until it enveloped the building, and all were engaged in prayer again. Andrew Murray tried to quiet the people walking up and down among them, but a stranger tiptoed to him and whispered: "I think that you are minister of this congregation. Be careful what you do, for it is the Spirit of God that is at work here." He said that he had recently arrived from America.[16]

Like many before him and after him, Murray realized that the Spirit of God moves as he wills (John 3:8). If Murray had continued to try to control or obstruct this divine outpouring, God would have bypassed him in order to accomplish his purposes. But Murray heeded the stranger's admonition and went from a posture of control to one of cooperation, and the results in his own life and throughout South Africa and beyond were extraordinary.

Movements shape history. I was privileged to be in London in June 2012 for a ceremony celebrating the 225th anniversary of the beginning of the movement to abolish the slave trade. The celebration was held in the church of St. Mary Woolnoth, the last parish in which John Newton (composer of "Amazing Grace") served as vicar before his death in 1807. In a nearby upper room, on June 21, 1787, twelve men met to form the Society for Effecting the Abolition of the Slave Trade (a sodality).

At the end of the evening celebrating this anniversary, we sang "Amazing Grace" a cappella, and it was as if the heavens opened. It was a profound experience to be in that place, which had been frequented by William Wilberforce and his colleagues, and to joyously participate in a celebration of perhaps the greatest movement for social change in the history of the Western world. Movements shape history, and few have been as powerful as the British abolitionists.

Movements deal with ultimate issues. Daniel Hudson Burnham, the famous architect, admonished others to "make no little plans. ... They have no magic to stir men's blood and probably themselves will not be realized."[17] It's the big plans that have the power and imagination to move people to action. Ultimate issues are the fuel of movements.

How tragic it is in our day to see so much energy and so many resources wasted on issues of no ultimate significance. Good things can often become enemies of the best things. And followers of Jesus are no less susceptible to a preoccupation with the insignificant than the rest of the world around us. As Floyd McClung puts it,

> We live in a world of competing passions. If we do not die to self and fill our lives with the consuming passion of the worship of God in the nations, we will end up with other passions. It's possible to deceive ourselves into thinking we have Biblical passions when, in reality, all we have done is to baptize the values of our culture and give them Christian names.[18]

Movements are characterized by discontent, vision and action. Psychologist Abraham Maslow's work on discontent shows us that in healthy organizations—and in human affairs in general— there are "high-order grumbles" that extend beyond the self to altruistic concerns for self or society. The paradox is that improvement does not necessarily bring contentment; rather the discontent just moves to a higher order of sophistication.

If we use Maslow's paradigm as a template, we realize that good movement leaders recognize that discontent is endemic. It's normal. And the quality of the discontent may say something about the quality of the movement and its leadership. Good movement leaders know how to move people from low-order discontent to higher-order discontent—and that's the stuff that fuels a movement. People aren't willing to die for the low-level stuff.[19]

Movements influence society from the bottom up, and move from the receptive to the resistant. Alan Hirsch writes that "movements are fluid, adaptive, and open to risks, and almost always begin in the grassroots of society."[20] Missiologist Donald McGavran goes to great lengths to describe and validate this idea. McGavran devotes an entire chapter to these dynamics—the gospel moving "from the masses to the classes"—in his book *Understanding Church Growth*. "One of the key questions on which mission policy hinges is this: Should we seek to win the upper classes first, confident that if we do they will win the lower classes . . . ? But for the most part, the strategy of winning the upper classes first has not worked. They will not be won."[21]

McGavran goes on to describe the importance of evaluating receptivity and resistance, regardless of class distinction, and states that "those who stand with arms outstretched, whether of the classes or the masses, have a higher right to hear than those who stop their ears and turn away" (Luke 9:5; 10:10-12).[22]

Apostolic structures and the movements they generate are not businesses, although there are important observations that can be made by comparing these parallel organizational structures. See table 9.1.

Movements are inherently nonconformist and even rebellious—they focus on change. If we are serious about starting movements, we have to realize that the best people to lead them are most likely nonconformists, dissenters and rebels. Mobilize the rebels and you'll get a movement. And usually the best place to find such rebels is on the fringes and the outskirts of organized religious institutions. They don't do as well in left-footed, local church or denominational settings.

Table 9.1

Characteristic	Movement of God	Business/Organization
Guiding documents	☐ beliefs ☐ values ☐ purpose ☐ vision	☐ strategic plans ☐ policies
Purpose	☐ otherworldly ☐ non-monetary	☐ profit and the bottom line
Motivation	☐ higher calling than return on monetary investment ☐ intangible/otherworldly rewards	☐ a paycheck—"here and now" compensation ☐ sense of personal fulfillment
Optimal way leaders lead	☐ spiritual authority	☐ positional authority ☐ competent authority
Structure	☐ organic/relational	☐ corporate, "businesslike"
Organizational dynamic	☐ challenging to lead ☐ morphs constantly ☐ culturally flexible ☐ socially adaptable ☐ geographically mobile	☐ structurally depends on context ☐ varying degrees of flexibility and adaptability
Market	☐ shapes the market, does not just respond to it ☐ values and calling transcend the market ☐ bends the market to a transcendent perspective by speaking prophetically	☐ responds to supply and demand and what will enhance the bottom line
Finances	☐ always on the edge ☐ rarely enough resources ☐ vision often outpaces supply lines	☐ if successful, is flush with money and resources
Relationship to the surrounding culture	☐ adapts its message without changing its core ☐ changes, challenges and confronts the culture	☐ reflects the culture

However, apostolic leaders—who are often inherently rebels at heart—must ensure that the rebels they recruit and lead are sanctified in their means as well as their ends. One of the greatest challenges for any apostolic leader is making sure that the compelling nature of the cause does not trump the character required of those who lead.

Movements are messy and chaotic. In his book *Thriving on*

Chaos, North American business guru Tom Peters captures principles that point the way forward in the turbulent business environment of a global economy. It's interesting that many of Peter's exhortations are not all that new to those familiar with movement dynamics. He says what lies ahead belongs to "the flexible, porous, adaptive, fleet-of-foot organization of the future: every person is 'paid' to be obstreperous, a disrespecter of formal boundaries, to hustle and to be fully engaged with engendering swift action, constantly improving everything."[23] And elsewhere, Peters writes, "Today, loving change, tumult, even chaos is a prerequisite for survival, let alone success."[24]

What Peters advocates can be observed in virtually every movement in Christianity past and present. It's an apostolic dynamic. And the environment surrounding those movements often appears to observers as what Peters calls "purposeful chaos."[25]

Movements can be diluted by an undue emphasis on excellence. Organizational consultant James Galvin makes an interesting argument about the paralyzing effect that the pursuit of excellence can have on a movement. "Organizational decline can be an unforeseen consequence of focusing on excellence. . . . Movements that obsess over refining existing methods to the exclusion of innovating for the future will eventually begin to decline. Leaders of declining movements change the conversation to survival, tradition, and heritage."[26]

Striving for excellence can come in many forms, not all of which are good for the health and momentum of a movement. In my experience, excellence is paralyzing most often when well-meaning people consider integrity and doing things "right" to be the highest priority. Of course, this gets tricky depending on whose definition of *right* is being used. When excellence is used as a synonym for perfectionism, the results can be debilitating.

Accountants, auditors, lawyers and human resource experts all excel in being enforcers of excellence. In the latter half of the twentieth century, a massive compliance industry emerged in North America to ensure that businesses—as well as nonprofits and religious organizations—toe the line on legal, personnel and financial matters.

In the realm of religious organizations, the admonition of Romans 13 regarding submission to the governing authorities and the law has driven ministry toward compliance with certain cultural standards of excellence. However, that passage can also unfortunately and unfairly be used as a club to stunt and subvert the freedom of movements to flourish. We need to understand the distinction between what is legal and what is moral, and we need to have an ongoing conversation about when submission to God trumps submission to earthly authority.

If some contemporary standards of excellence had been enforced in the post-Pentecost days of the book of Acts, the apostolic movement that exploded throughout the Roman world in the following centuries would have been stymied. Contemporary concepts of accountability and excellence are an invention of modernity, and they can be destructive when applied bluntly to spiritual movements. Movements can be co-opted by the prevailing culture and an obsession with excellence can have a subtle, yet very real, stifling effect on what the Spirit of God is doing in our time. "If the word 'excellence' is to be applicable in the future, it requires some redefinition. Perhaps: 'Excellent firms don't believe in excellence—only in constant improvement and constant change.' That is, the excellent firms of tomorrow will cherish impermanence—and thrive on chaos."[27]

Movements should only appoint and retain leaders who are fully committed to the movement's beliefs and practices. Being part of a movement can be painful. The relational toll can be costly. Consequently, it's not uncommon in leadership selection and succession for movements to gravitate toward people who will be less controversial, less demanding, more pastoral and easier to get along with than the initial apostolic provocateurs who launched the movement. How a movement navigates such choices and transitions will help determine the longevity of the movement and its ultimate impact. I've personally seen gifted apostolic leaders sacrificed on the altar of care and concern, and the calling of God to accomplish an urgent task overridden by the need for relational peace.

I was sitting over a cup of coffee with one of CRM's senior leaders, who had many years of ministry experience. I was disappointed to hear him say, "I'm done. I don't want to be part of a movement. Where you're headed is not where I want to go."

When he said that, I knew his tenure with us was over. There was no future for him in an organization whose stated aim is so clearly movement-focused. God could certainly have other significant plans for his future; maybe it was time for a new direction in his ministry. But the worst thing I could have done for him—and for those in an organization filled with people mutually called to catalyzing and multiplying movements—would have been to keep him on board out of a sense of compassion or because of our long-standing relationship.

There are two dynamics that have to be balanced and reconciled in successful movements. One is task, and the other is relationships. *Both* are essential and often coexist with great tension in the pursuit of mission. Hirsch and Frost are right when they say that "Mission is a task! It defines us and gives God's people their distinctive and irreplaceable direction and purpose."[28] But at the same time, people are the focus of Jesus' love and redemptive passion, and as the parable of the lost sheep teaches us, the priority and dignity of the one is never lost in the midst of the many.

Good leadership is able to weave both of these emphases together, and to create an environment where individuals can be valued for their own unique contributions while simultaneously giving themselves wholeheartedly to something bigger than themselves.

Local churches are not movements. I believe the term *church planting movements*, often heard in mission circles, can be a bit misleading. The term implies that local churches can multiply spontaneously and on their own. While we certainly want to embed a DNA in all local churches that encourages them to multiply (particularly in their own near-neighbor contexts), it is incredibly difficult for them to multiply *on their own*. The very local church structures that we have created in the Western world—highly institutionalized and traditional—make such multiplication doubly difficult.

When movements take off most effectively, both sodalities and modalities are always involved. Invariably, apostolic people and the necessary apostolic structures to facilitate the movement are in the mix. "Wherever and whenever the church has significantly extended the mission of God or experienced rapid growth there has always been apostolic leadership present in some form or another."[29]

In any movement, apostolic people and organizations serve three critical functions:

1. They act as catalysts: they create and kick-start movements.

2. They inject vision, commitment and energy into movements at critical junctures to sustain momentum.

3. They play a critical role in the development of leadership—an essential component for the ongoing health and vitality of movements.

These contributions are most effective when apostolic people and organizations are able to maintain their God-given distinction from the church in its local form. Distinctives must be held and distance maintained. When the right-foot, left-foot analogy is lived out in practice—when right feet work alongside and in healthy interdependence with left feet—the result is a powerful structural synergy that propels a movement forward.

Sometimes local churches may work together and pool their resources as part of a larger connectional structure. Depending on church polity, these cooperative arrangements can be anything from loose networks or associations to highly sophisticated denominations.

However, without strong relationships with apostolic people and apostolic structures, associations of local churches—whether networks or denominations—lose a powerful force that can help prevent their slide toward ossification.

Sometimes these networks or denominations may work cooperatively to form their own internal apostolic structures. That's what denominational mission agencies are. But if there is any hope for movements to occur, these apostolic structures must be given an appropriate amount of freedom to operate apart from the control of denominational hierarchies and bureaucracies. Just like physical running, the key to effective ongoing movements is both the left and right feet working interdependently.

Movements build strong ties between members for mutual support and accountability. As James MacGregor Burns famously said, "Any movement which has benefited society in the long haul has at its core a group of people committed to a cause that they consider greater than themselves and to one another as friends."

Relationships can never be the ultimate focus of a movement. They are never an adequate substitute for vision. However, one of the essential components for momentum in a movement is its relationships. After many years of experience I have come to embrace the fact that movements run on relationships more than any other human factor. I cannot think of a single movement, be it religious, social or political, where there was not a profound relational dynamic at its core.

In any healthy movement, then, participants should be able to answer some important questions.

1. Where is the relational nexus of the movement?

2. What is my contribution to the relational dynamic?

3. What is done, intentionally and inadvertently, to nourish this relational dynamic?

4. What or who is detracting from the relational synergy, and how are the negative contributions being minimized?

5. Who are the key players in the relational mix? Who stewards the relational component of the movement?

6. Are the relationships based on the two components that Burns articulates—a cause and friendship?

Momentum in any movement is a precious commodity. It's hard to get, and it's easy to lose. But one of the primary components of acquiring and sustaining momentum has always been and always will be relationships.

The methods in a movement may change, but the cause never does. When we orient new personnel at CRM, we strive to make this principle very clear. Our essentials don't change: mission, vision, values and basic beliefs. However, we embrace and even celebrate great diversity methodologically, culturally and geographically. As Steve Addison describes it,

> Adaptive methods are the scaffolding of a movement, not the building itself. They remind us that the kingdom of heaven must be grounded in everyday practicalities. A living organism cannot survive without effective systems that can adapt to different environments. The good news of Jesus Christ is unchanging and eternal, yet its form must continually change in response to each situation. Our methods must serve our message by ensuring that the gospel can spread unhindered across cultural and geographic boundaries.[30]

Movements are supremely adaptable and flexible. They are prepared to change anything except their core beliefs.

I am deeply grateful for the formative role that J. Robert Clinton played in my life as a personal mentor and friend for many years.[31] He also served for two decades on CRM's governing board, and his wisdom helped shape and steer us through growing pains and difficult times. I remember a meeting I had with Bobby during which we discussed how to generate and sustain momentum in movements. His admonition to me as a leader was to do whatever was necessary to maintain flexibility. "Missionary teams and structures must be nimble," he said. "Guard your freedom to respond quickly to needs. Be ready to alter course on the spur of the moment, and make spontaneous corrections in response to change."

Movements make demands on their followers. Movements demand sacrifice. Dean Kelley was a researcher commissioned by the National Council of Churches in 1972 to do a sociological study on why the more theologically liberal, mainline denominations in North America were stagnant or declining while the conservative, evangelical bodies were apparently thriving. The result of Kelley's research was the landmark study, *Why Conservative Churches Are Growing: A Study in Sociology of Religion.*[32]

What Kelley found was not surprising. Those who made serious demands on the beliefs and behavior of their people thrived. Those who only expected their people to be "reasonable, rational, courteous, responsible, restrained and receptive to outside criticism . . . gentle and democratic" struggled. They were advocating a recipe for the failure of the religious enterprise, which arose from a mistaken view of what success is and how it should be fostered and measured.

New York Times columnist David Brooks reiterates the same critique. "Vague, uplifting, non-doctrinal religiosity doesn't actually last. The religions that grow, succor and motivate people to perform heroic acts of service are usually theologically rigorous, arduous in practice and definite in their convictions about what is True and False." Brooks goes on to say that "regular acts of discipline can lay the foundation for extraordinary acts of self-control when it counts the most."[33]

If we are committed to furthering the movement that Jesus started, we should be serious about communicating the cost to people upfront. When I invite someone to follow Jesus, I make a habit of telling them why they should soberly consider such a decision, and I often point them to the words of Jesus in Luke 9:23: "Whoever wants to be my disciple must deny themselves and take up their cross daily and follow me." Following Jesus means embracing an instrument of death on a daily basis. Following Jesus will cost everything. As Dietrich Bonheoffer famously said, "When Christ calls a man, he bids him come and die."[34]

Calling people to Jesus' movement means calling them to sacrifice and even death. According to Jesus, nothing less will do.

Movements are at home in their host culture, but are radically distinct from it. An effective movement will be radically counter-cultural and culturally relevant at the same time. That's a curious but compelling paradox, which is also reflected in Scripture when Jesus prays for his disciples to be in the world but not of it (John 17:14-18). An effective movement will be able to communicate with stunning effectiveness without alienating people. It will draw them into its vortex as it brings about substantive change. As Steve Addison puts it, "The key to evangelicalism's vitality, then, is its ability to exist in tension with the surrounding culture while at the same time remaining engaged."[35]

On a practical level, this means living out a saying used in Accelerate training (we'll talk more about Accelerate below): *We want to be spiritually intoxicating, contagious and compelling without being religiously obnoxious.*

Profound encounters with God are the catalysts of movements. This is one of the ingredients Steve Addison describes in detail as being at the heart of every submovement within the overall Christian movement: "A white-hot faith obsessed with the Spirit, the Word and the World. . . . Fresh encounters with God through the Word and Spirit provide compelling authority that energizes a missionary movement to go and change the world."[36]

"The Apostolic Through the Ages" (available online) includes a long list of apostolic leaders and movements which spans the breadth of the two millennia since Pentecost.[37] If we dig deep enough, we will invariably find in each movement a person or group of persons who deeply encountered the living God.

The mission to which we have been called is like a destination on a map. We've been given a car that represents a movement. It's made up of components that must work together for the car to move smoothly and in the right direction. And it's a vehicle that we've been asked to drive. The gas that powers it is the presence and work of the Spirit of God, and it comes only from union and communion with Christ. The car goes nowhere without it.

The need of the hour is to "remonk" the church with apostolic leaders and the sodality structures in which they can thrive in cooperation with the local church. May God do exactly that, not just for the sake of his people, but for the sake of all those who are far from him, those whom he longs to draw into the freeing life of his kingly rule and the redeeming community of his kingdom.

And may he do it through those of you for whom this book is written: those apostolically gifted men and women destined to make your God-ordained contribution around the world through fresh, authentic gospel movements. May what is written here validate your calling and encourage you to action. The health and vibrancy of the entire Christian movement is at stake, and the eternal destiny of the multitudes hangs in the balance.

10

The Momentum of Movements

To kill or to multiply, that is the question

Thus, if his church wants to be faithful to his revelation, it will be completely mobile, fluid, renascent, bubbling, creative, inventive, adventurous, and imaginative. It will never be perennial, and can never be organized or institutionalized.

Jacques Ellul, *The Subversion of Christianity*

The great growth of the future is also likely to be by people movements. . . . The people movement is a God-given way by which social resistance to the gospel can be surmounted.

Donald McGavran, *Understanding Church Growth*

Without revolutionary theory, there can be no revolutionary movement.

Vladimir Lenin, *What Is to Be Done?*

The central focus of my personal calling—and of those with whom I have journeyed in lifelong ministry—is to see movements of fresh, authentic expressions of the gospel multiplied among the nations. In that pursuit I've also repeatedly observed what can discourage, stunt and even kill such movement momentum. Here is my list of movement killers.

1. Requiring formal education for the leadership.

2. Demanding conformity to methodology.

3. Refusing to provide the necessary administrative and logistical support, without which a movement will suffocate under its own weight.

4. Downplaying the validity of supernatural phenomena outside our paradigm.

5. Not allowing room for younger, less experienced leadership.

6. Being obsessed with theological purity.

7. Valuing the safety of the people involved more highly than the mission itself.

8. Centralizing the funding.

9. Punishing out-of-the-box thinking.

10. Managing instead of leading.

11. Rewarding faithfulness more than entrepreneurial ability.

12. Being tied to property and buildings.

13. Being defined by critics.

14. Being threatened by giftedness that's unlike our own.

15. Creating an endowment so there is no need to raise money.

16. Treating creativity as heresy.

17. Refusing to exercise discipline when it is needed.

18. Relying on existing institutions for credibility.

19. Promoting people on the basis of seniority and longevity.

20. Insisting that decisions be based on policy instead of values.

21. Focusing on nurture and the conservation of gains.

22. Not giving proper attention to the selection of leaders.

23. Being risk-averse under the guise of stewardship.

24. Justifying a reluctance to raise money.

25. Recruiting people who have a big need for approval and affirmation.

26. And above all else, trying to control the movement of the Spirit when he actually shows up!

ACCELERATE

One of the most powerful approaches I've seen to catalyzing contemporary apostolic movements is called "Accelerate." [1] This is an international team within CRM but with a reach and involvement that includes many other global partners. The primary pioneer for Accelerate has been David Broodryk from South Africa.

Accelerate is a fresh expression of initiatives in the missions world, sometimes referred to as "Church Planting Movements" or "Disciple Making Movements." Building on these foundations, Accelerate focuses specifically on urban areas and provides highly effective evangelism and discipleship processes to create and sustain gospel movements. It is a philosophy of ministry I am personally committed to implementing.

The primary laboratory for my own understanding of the Disciple Making Movement processes that Accelerate uses has been the Middle East and North Africa. Within a period of just a few years in that region, we have seen a phenomenal number of people moving toward an obedient and living faith in Jesus. Some are coming from nominal Christian backgrounds. Most are Muslims. But these movements throughout the region far exceed anything that I could ever have imagined possible within my lifetime. They have the potential to change the course of history in this volatile region of the world. They are real. They are deep. They are substantial.

Alim leads one such movement in North Africa. He has implemented Disciple Making Movement processes among the handicapped and disabled and their families, and the results have been astonishing. Within an eighteen-month period, he saw 130 discovery groups planted. These groups, averaging fifteen to twenty-five people per group, were made up of people far from God who were willing to discuss stories from the Bible. Alim told me that the good news of Jesus spreads like wildfire among these families, and people who have been socially shunned for years are coming out of the shadows.

After many months of watching groups form and multiply, Alim finally began to gather people from different groups together, and he showed me a video of one such event—about 250 people in a room rented in a school: people in wheelchairs, walking on crutches, being carried, some with physical and others with intellectual disabilities. The man leading worship for the group was blind. It is truly a movement among the forgotten. As my wife says, "The pleasure of God drenches this group!"

As these kinds of movements have taken root and multiplied around the world, they have been blessed by obscurity. In China, India, East Africa and now in the Middle East, movements with similar components at their heart have been "under the radar"— which has contributed to their health and sustainability. Little has been written about them, and in some contexts they are called different things. One account is the book *Miraculous Movements*, which describes the incredible movement of God in the Horn of Africa.[2] *The Father Glorified* is another overview of these dynamics.[3]

Depending on whom we ask and how we track, there are at least 150 such movements at the time this book is being written that are verifiable and ongoing, catalyzed by a plethora of apostolic people and organizations. One of the qualifying characteristics used in this data is that there must be at least four generations of group multiplication evident, and some have even been tracked beyond fifteen generations.

Such a blessed lack of notoriety is also advantageous as these movements gain traction in the Western world. It would be tragic for such organic processes to be packaged, systematized and marketed in the West. Selling Accelerate as the latest cure-all on the never-ending North American conference circuit would be a deathblow. The tools and processes employed in Accelerate need to be implemented, not publicized.

TEACHING TO OBEY

The Disciple Making Movement processes and tools used in Accelerate are effective because they

- disciple people to conversion, and not the other way around
- focus on obedience
- depend on the transforming power of the Bible and the manifest presence of the Holy Spirit—a rather unbeatable combination
- are simple and highly reproducible
- have rapid multiplication built into their essential DNA from the very beginning
- are highly relational and organic
- depend on the ability of people to discover truth for themselves—there are no preachers, teachers or experts in the beginning stages

Christianity in the West has long been characterized by its orientation to knowledge and information. It's not obedience that counts; it's what we know. Consequently, we have systematically taught people how to be less than obedient to God by the very forms of spirituality and paradigms of growth we embrace. The processes in Accelerate turn that paralyzing set of presuppositions on its head and take John 14:21 seriously: "Whoever has my commands and keeps them is the one who loves me . . . and I too will love them and show myself to them." It puts legs under Jesus' final command in Matthew 28:20 to teach them "to obey everything I have commanded you."

Doug and Colletta are North Americans who now live in one of the sprawling townships outside Pretoria, South Africa—a black African landscape. Doug and Colletta have crossed significant racial and cultural barriers to gain trust and acceptance, and while their presence certainly speaks to reconciliation, that's not their primary focus. Rather, they are there to implement Accelerate processes and catalyze gospel movements that will multiply in the township and beyond. And it's happening. People are becoming disciples of Jesus who are committed to making more disciples. Groups are multiplying. Movement momentum has begun. Profound cultural and social change will result, because people are following and obeying Jesus.

MOVEMENTS IN THE WEST

I believe Accelerate tools and processes can be powerfully relevant in the secularized world of postmodernity in the West. I know of few better ways in the West to shift us from our stifling posture of religious maintenance back into genuine, authentic missionality.

Accelerate uniquely addresses the increasing neo-barbarism of Western culture—similar to the way the Celtic movement connected so powerfully with the pagan cultures into which it moved—much more effectively than the head-oriented, nonexperiential intellectualism to which most of us in the West are accustomed. As of this writing, we are beginning to see real traction, albeit embryonic, as Accelerate is implemented in places like Sacramento and Boston, Long Beach and Spokane. We are also seeing results in Western Europe, in places as diverse as St. Petersburg and London.

Elements of Accelerate can also be adapted for institutional local church settings.[4] However, the nature of the local church in the West can make it a difficult context for such ministry to flourish, because Accelerate inevitably generates a different church paradigm than what has predominated since the time of Constantine.

I believe Accelerate has the best potential for traction when it is initiated by people in apostolic structures and exercised among people who are far from God. Such apostolicity is essential for the ongoing multiplication of such movements and is particularly needed for leadership development at critical hinge points.

Phil had initially been a pastor and denominational leader, but in midlife he made the jump to a missionary vocation. Shortly afterward, he began to apply Accelerate processes and tools. Through a unique set of circumstances, he began to implement this type of ministry among people incarcerated in the large public prison system of a state in the American Midwest. After Phil initially and providentially found persons of peace in the system,[5] first one discovery Bible study started (sometimes called discovery groups), then a second, then a third, and within three years, hundreds of groups had started. Soon over three hundred inmates had come to a living, vibrant faith in Jesus.

The movement expanded outside the walls of the prisons and spread through the families and homes of those incarcerated, and over fifteen generations of groups multiplied. To this day, we continue to see an expanding movement of the gospel in this prison system and beyond. No preachers or teachers to begin with. No experts. Through the quiet use of the Bible and the manifest presence of the Holy Spirit, hundreds of prisoners have become committed, obedient followers of Jesus. It's a genuine gospel movement.

When these new disciples are released from prison, do they end up participating in existing churches on the outside? Do their families gravitate to traditional churches? Some do. But many don't. They've tasted and experienced authentic spirituality and the presence of God without some of the trappings of Christendom, and consequently their needs are met in groups just like they experienced in prison. They enjoy new forms and expressions of church that include all of the biblical functions, but may not look much like the surrounding religious institutions and traditional church culture.

MULTIPLYING IN HARD PLACES

Sajid had been a pastor in a city in the Middle East for eighteen years, a world away from the American Midwest. During that time, he had started two churches using methods he'd learned by observing and being trained by missionaries from the West. Through a lot of blood, sweat and tears, two healthy congregations were established: one with about fifty people and another with thirty, which by Middle Eastern standards was very successful. But it had taken over a decade and a half.

Then Sajid was exposed to the Disciple Making Movement philosophy of ministry, and when he began to implement it his world was turned upside down. Sajid became part of an apostolic team that has seen somewhere in excess of twenty thousand people find new life in Christ within five years. These are not raised hands in a crusade or public meeting, but individuals deeply immersed in the Bible and determined to obey Jesus regardless of the cost. They are people committed to one another and growing together in new expressions of church appropriate to their context. The level of commitment is as high as in Sajid's original two churches— and they have the martyrs to prove it.

Like Phil, Sajid is on the ground floor of a genuine gospel

movement from which new expressions of the church are emerging. The problem with examples like these is that the data almost immediately becomes obsolete.

I was in a cramped apartment in a Middle Eastern city, observing a group of twenty people who had fled from the atrocities of the Syrian civil war. They were animated as they discussed a story about Jesus—what it told them about God, what it told them about people, and if it was true, what must they do. As with Phil and Sajid's experiences, there were no teachers, no preachers—just people far from God but willing to listen to stories from the Bible and consider what to do in response.

I learned that usually all those who participate weekly in these kinds of groups become committed followers of Jesus within four to six months. And groups like this were meeting around the clock in this apartment. It was a struggle to accommodate everyone who wanted to participate. Hundreds of groups had multiplied among the refugees in this city, and the momentum was growing.

MULTIPLYING MOVEMENTS = MULTIPLYING STRUCTURES

> It is astonishing that most Protestant missionaries . . . have been blind to the significance of the very structure within which they have worked. In this blindness they have merely planted churches and have not effectively concerned themselves to make sure that the kind of mission structure within which they operate also be set up on the field.[6]

We cannot multiply only right-footed *people*. We also need to multiply the right-footed *structures* that are tailored to them and in which they can thrive. After a decade of work in dozens of nations where resident missionaries had been sent, CRM came face-to-face with this challenge. First, how seriously were we taking Winter's admonition? Second, what kinds of apostolic structures best accommodate the unique needs of right-footed people?

Responding to the first question meant rethinking what our end was in the crosscultural context in which we were ministering. If the end was making disciples, developing leaders and generating movements, what we were doing was inadequate. We would not be successful and faithful to God's calling unless we also multiplied the apostolic structures from which we ourselves had been sent. Right-footed people and right-footed structures go hand-in-hand. In crosscultural contexts, this meant creating indigenous structures in which

- nationals called to apostolic ministry could serve and thrive

- nationals would control and lead

- nationals were sending themselves to new crosscultural venues and replicating the same process

Several strategic questions were important to answer. First, how would these apostolic entities relate to one another? We decided to set up these structures in what is commonly called a distributive organization. This means the structures relate to one another in a fraternal, nonobligatory manner, where each entity stands on its own. There is no centralized control. It is not like the Vatican or like older missionary structures, with a headquarters or a center of authority.

Second, we determined that we needed a structure in which people and resources could flow freely across international, cultural and linguistic barriers. We needed a structure that would facilitate a global learning community.

Third, we wanted to learn from the mistakes of the church in the past regarding the use of money and resources in missions. How could we move away from the often unhealthy dependence throughout the global church on Western financial resources and yet still raise the necessary support, regardless of where the resources are generated?

CONEXT

The result of these conversations was CoNext—a fraternal partnership of likeminded, apostolic organizations committed to the same basic beliefs, vision, mission and values. It's a right-footed partnership for right-footed structures. As of this writing, CoNext is represented in a dozen countries: Venezuela, South Korea, the United Kingdom, Hungary, several countries in the Middle East, Nigeria, South Africa, Ukraine, Australia, the United States and Canada, with more to come.

My airline of choice is United because it connects easily to many of the locations that I need to reach. But United is part of a global airline partnership called Star Alliance. Star Alliance is a good illustration of the kind of global partnership CoNext is for these apostolic organizations. Each airline has its own separate identity. Each stands or falls on its own business plan and bottom line. If one fails, it may have repercussions for the others, but the health and survival of the group is not dependent on any one of the partners. It's a classic example of the organizational structure made famous by Ori Brafman and Rod Beckstrom in their book, *The Starfish and the Spider*.[7]

We've structured CoNext in a way that enables us to freely move and share people and resources. For example, when North Americans are sent to Hungary to be part of our Hungarian partner, *Barnabas Csoport* ("the Barnabas Group"), the North Americans are seconded to the Hungarians. They submit to Hungarian leadership and report to nationals.

Each national entity is likewise responsible to fund those who are sent from their country or people group. That does not mean that the money necessarily comes directly from that country, but that the national leadership bears the responsibility to fund their own missionaries. The money may come from any global source.

CoNext is a work in progress. We are learning as we go. How much structure is too much? How little is too little? How can we balance the immense diversity between languages, cultures and con-

texts, and still maintain a clear vision and a unified purpose? These
are all good questions with corresponding challenges. But in the end,
all of us who lead CoNext partner organizations agree that our
purpose is to generate and multiply movements and, in partnership
with all those local churches that already exist or need to be created,
capitalize on a dynamic that has extraordinary potential.

AN ORDER AMONG THE POOR

A good case study of multiplying apostolic structures is Inner-
CHANGE, a part of CRM.[8] As an order among the poor, Inner-
CHANGE is an excellent example of contemporary remonking,
and as of this writing, over 125 men and women live and minister
as part of InnerCHANGE teams in a dozen major urban contexts
worldwide. As a neo-monastic order, they make commitments
(take vows), live in close proximity to one another and practice
communal rhythms in their life together.

The focus of InnerCHANGE is to make disciples of Jesus among
the poor and to multiply gospel movements among the marginalized. What is unique about InnerCHANGE is the way they go
about this—by living incarnationally among those the world has
overlooked and forgotten, those who are the least among us
(Matthew 25:40). This is not a "drive in, drive out" philosophy of
ministry. These missionaries live out the presence of Jesus in poor
communities in word, deed and power.

From the barrios of Caracas to the dense urban sprawl of South
Asia, these apostolic entrepreneurs live and serve among the poor.
They can be found serving with the homeless in the back alleys of
San Francisco, working with street kids in Guatemala, partnering
with church leaders in Cambodia, living in the townships of South
Africa and with international refugees in Minneapolis.

InnerCHANGE is part of an informal network of apostolic
structures called New Friars, made up of similar apostolic organiza-

tions such as Word Made Flesh, Servant Partners and Urban Neighborhoods of Hope. Fixed squarely in the tradition of earlier sodalities such as the Franciscans, the Moravians and the Jesuits, these contemporary neo-monastics include Catholics and Protestants, men and women, and they do not require celibacy.[9]

IN THE FINAL ANALYSIS

In the latter half of the twentieth century, the Christian movement became a truly global phenomenon for the first time in history. This does not mean that every culture or people group has been effectively reached or has healthy expressions of the church within it. Far from it. But it does mean that in 2011, the 2.18 billion self-identified Christians worldwide represented nearly one-third of the world's total population of 6.9 billion. And these people who share some level of allegiance to Christ "are also geographically widespread—so far flung, in fact, that no single continent or region can indisputably claim to be the center of global Christianity. A century ago, this was not the case. Christianity today, unlike a century ago, is truly a global faith."[10]

But this great shift did not happen without intentionality. On the contrary, it is primarily a result of the great Protestant missionary movement of the nineteenth and twentieth centuries. What we see worldwide today is the result of a countless array of apostolic people living out their calling, working in harmony with left-footed church structures, faithfully and sacrificially making disciples of Jesus among the nations.

This global movement is indebted to many diverse pioneers. In China, people like James O. Fraser, Charles Gordon, Isobel Kuhn, Lottie Moon and Hudson Taylor led the way. Other pioneers include Barclay Buxton in Japan, John Geddie in Oceania, Adoniram Judson in Burma and Amy Carmichael, E. Stanley Jones, Donald McGavran, Sadhu Singh and St. Teresa of Calcutta in India.

In other areas of Asia, Charles Cowan, D. E. Hoste, Robert Jaffray,

Eric Liddell and Robert Morrison led the way. In the Middle East, Henry Martyn, Douglas Thornton and Samuel Zwemer were examples of sacrificial apostolic leadership. And in Latin America there were Jim Elliot, Kenneth Strachan and Cam Townsend.

In Africa, men and women like David Livingstone, Helen Roseveare, William Shepherd, Mary Slessor and C. T. Studd lived out apostolic passion. Apostolic pioneers in the Western world include Lyman Beecher, Samuel Brengle, William Bright, Loren Cunningham, Ted Fletcher, F. B. Meyer, John R. Mott, Florence Nightingale, Bob Pierce, A. T. Pierson, Jim Rayburn, Charles Simeon, A. B. Simpson, Dawson Trotman, John Wesley, Ralph Winter and many others.

This brief list of apostolic heroes and heroines is the tiniest tip of a massive iceberg. Many who deserve a place in such an apostolic hall of fame lived, labored and died in blessed obscurity. Today, rough estimates suggest that from all branches of Christendom, approximately four hundred and thirty thousand men and women work as missionaries—second decision people serving in right-footed structures—of which one hundred and forty thousand are Protestant. But their impact in relationship to the 2.18 billion professing Christians worldwide is proportionally extraordinary.

The current global success of the greater Christian movement is due in large part to these apostolic people working through apostolic structures, creating movement after movement within the greater whole. These are God's pioneers accomplishing God's purposes through God-ordained structures.

The worldwide health, multiplication and vibrancy of the Christian movement that has occurred over the past two centuries would have never occurred without them. Apostolic people and apostolic structures are a biblical, historical and missiological necessity, and where they thrive, the blessing of God is abundantly evident.

Conclusion

Be a history shaper

*If you have apostolic passion, you are one of the
most dangerous people on the planet.*

Floyd McClung, "Apostolic Passion"

*The greatest danger for most of us is not that our aim is too high
and we miss it, but that it is too low and we reach it.*

Michelangelo

*Get out in the stream of history and
swim as fast as you can.*

William O. Douglas

A t the very core of every gospel movement from Pentecost
onward there have been people with apostolic calling and
passion, boldly living it out in apostolic structures that go beyond
the local church.

Perhaps you are one of those people. While you are appreciative of local churches—you may have grown up in one—you realize that there must be something more. God has placed a holy unsettledness inside you and a fire to press the boundaries of kingdom exploration. You suffer from restlessness and an entrepreneurial drive that lives, breathes and longs for adventure beyond local ecclesiological boundaries.

I hope this book has given you a sound basis for your calling and substantiated your legitimacy. That zeal in your heart is from God. You are valid and so are the apostolic teams or organizations that can give you a platform and a means to pursue the dreams entrusted to you by heaven.

Thankfully, you are part of a new and growing generation that is emerging with a holistic and fully orbed missional ecclesiology. Based on solid theology, the testimony of history and proven missiology, you are among the men and women who have an extraordinary opportunity to live out their apostolic calling in a way that will be a blessing to the nations. May your numbers multiply and your fervency increase.

You stand on the shoulders of giants who, sometimes unrecognized in their own time, have been the foundation of many succeeding generations of gospel pioneers and the catalysts of apostolic movements for the past two thousand years. Often behind the scenes, unnoticed and insignificant by the standards of the religious establishments around them, these apostolic people and the movements they have spawned and multiplied have shaped the course of history.

What's thrilling is that such movements are not just historical. While we can celebrate the thousands of missionary saints who have gone before, it's happening in our own time as well.

David is South African, and over a fifteen-year period, he planted four churches in the northern part of the nation using crusade methodology. These new churches averaged about eighty people per congregation. David was committed to church planting because he believed it was one of the best ways to see people far from God become followers of Jesus. And David is an apostolically gifted leader.

Over a decade and a half, the church planting process took a grueling toll on David's family, his health and his finances. Just at the point when he was ready to give it all up out of discouragement, he was introduced to a whole new way to conceive of church and a radically different vision of how to introduce people to Jesus. It was all about gospel movements—not just planting a church or seeing a person become a follower of Jesus.

So in the midst of the fifth church plant, David took the bold move of closing it down and, with about half of the participants, dove headlong into implementing a movement strategy—what we know now as Accelerate—as a missionary, not a pastor. He pioneered ground that was beyond the reach of the local church and where existing local expressions could not or would not go.

Eight years later, the results are nothing less than amazing. Over twenty-five hundred new churches have been multiplied, averaging around forty participants in size. And over eighty thousand people from nonbelieving backgrounds have now become committed followers of Jesus.

David's role is highly apostolic in nature and transcends denominations. He and his team are the catalysts, the coaches, the mentors and the trainers alongside the gospel movement that has emerged and is flourishing across southern Africa. They don't pastor. They don't publically teach. They don't preach. But within this robust movement, indigenous pastoral leadership has emerged as the movement has matured. It is a thrilling example of apostolic leaders working in tandem with burgeoning church expressions, all combined into a powerful gospel movement.

Frankly, I hesitate to tell such stories because I know the incredulity such numbers can generate, particularly in the Western world. But David's story is not unique. There are at least another hundred and fifty such movements documented that I could point to spread all over the world. Many are in restricted-access countries and exist below the radar, and going public with specifics could seriously jeopardize the leaders and the movements. But I've seen some of these movements up close and personal on different continents and in varying cultural contexts.

The point is that these things work! Movements *are* possible. It's not just theory. It's real. And at the heart of such movements are always apostolic people, willing to buck the status quo and move beyond personal peace and safety, women and men anxious for a life of sacrifice and authenticity, determined "to boldly go where no one has gone before."

Ultimately, however, we must look one layer below the concepts of apostolicity and movements and ask, "Why?" What's so sacrosanct about movements? The answer is that behind the concept of movements is a driving passion for the nations and a heart that breaks for people far from Jesus.

No one will ever develop a passion about movements without a passion first for the whole world to follow the living Christ and welcome his kingdom presence. Movements are a means to a much greater end—the glory of God among the nations, that the name of Jesus may be honored, loved and obeyed and that his name may be renowned among all the peoples of the earth.

As John Piper so powerfully writes: "All of history is moving toward one great goal, the white-hot worship of God and his Son among all the peoples of the earth. Missions is not that goal. It is the means. And for that reason it is the second greatest activity in the world."[1]

May God graciously make it so in our day, and may each of us step into the part that he has for us in this grand adventure.

Acknowledgments

This book was written during a five-month sabbatical in 2013, which I took with the gracious encouragement of the CRM-US Board of Directors. The men and women who serve on this body have always epitomized the very best in organizational governance, and it is a joy to be accountable to people of this caliber and godly character. They have always "watched out for my soul" and I am profoundly grateful.

The sabbatical would not have been possible had it not been for the team that gives daily leadership and oversight to the staff and teams of CRM-US spread out around the world. Too many to mention, they are exemplary models of apostolic leadership, and the people whom they lead are those referred to in the poem at the end of chapter seven: "the great ones of this generation of whom the world is not worthy."

Many people have built into my life over the years, but two especially deserve mention. Early on, Chuck Singletary was my Barnabas. He believed in me, risked in recruiting me for apostolic ministry and sponsored me into leadership and responsibility far beyond my experience. What he imparted to me was the inestimable value of believing in people and trusting them, and he gave me freedom to soar. If I am able to pass that on to future generations it is because Chuck lived it and demonstrated it toward me.

And the contribution of J. Robert Clinton—the indomitable professor of leadership at Fuller Seminary whom we all know as "Bobby"—is beyond significant. His understanding and insight into leadership seem almost second nature to me, and they have been deeply imbedded in the ethos and organizational culture of CRM around the globe.

I am grateful to both of these men as mentors and as friends, and I believe that all of us serving with CRM are a substantial part of their legacies.

Thank you to early peers who were powerful forces to shape my lifelong values, direction and missional passion. Many of those relationships were formed when I was a student at the University of Virginia in the context of The Navigators, one of the twentieth century's prime examples of an apostolic sodality. That was where I learned the Bible—not just the importance of knowing the Bible but the imperative of obeying it.

In recent years, I've been thankful for the ministry assistants God has entrusted to me. They've put up with thousands of miles of travel in dozens of countries and cultures and have been subjected to endless conversations and processing, helping me refine and communicate what this book espouses. Thank you, Tom, Travis, Josh and Jacob.

None of the ministry that Patty and I have been able to pursue over these decades would have been possible apart from the generosity and partnership of our financial partners. May God return to these wonderful friends and churches many times over what you've shared with us. Even more important have been those faithful men and women who have been on our personal intercession teams. Behind the scenes, your contribution has moved mountains.

Many thanks to those God has used to encourage me and CRM toward normalizing supernatural reality in our ministry in recent days: John and Jill Kloos, Jim Hanley, Chuck Kraft, Barry and Mary Kissel, Verlie Hamilton, Colin and C'havala Crawley, Keith Uebele and Nadim Costa. Your gracious, unsensational ministry has influenced the writing of this volume and helped me understand that mere words without the anointing of God lack spiritual power and authenticity. I am so grateful.

I am indebted to those national leaders who are part of the CoNext partnership. Together, we have an opportunity to model the multiplying of apostolic sodalities across cultures and among the nations. We've only scratched the surface of putting into practice what this book is all about.

A variety of people have made this volume much more valuable than it would have been if left solely up to me. Pauline Kirke, Lori Larson, Michelle Klewer and Christine Aanderud put in many tedious hours of research and fine tuning the details of the manuscript. Al Hsu at IVP provided invaluable editorial guidance that substantially improved the text and kept me from offending more people than necessary.

I am indebted to my family: David and Christine (and their spouses, Meredith and Danny). You've lived through four decades of ministry with me as this book was hammered out in the crucible of real life. You've seen all my flaws and foibles up close and personal. My prayer is for you and for every generation that follows to be passionate followers of Jesus. And to Patty, my spouse and best friend, who is equally gifted and called as I am to a life of apostolic abandonment. None of what's written in these pages could have been tested and tried without your support, partnership and love.

Notes

FOREWORD

[1]Joshua Cooper Ramo, *The Age of the Unthinkable: Why the New World Disorder Constantly Surprises Us and What We Can Do About It* (New York: Little, Brown and Company, 2009).

[2]See Alan Hirsch and Michael Frost, *The Faith of Leap: Embracing a Theology of Adventure and Risk* (Grand Rapids: Baker, 2013), pp. 153-54.

INTRODUCTION

[1]Rodney Clapp, "Remonking the Church: Would a Protestant Form of Monasticism Help Liberate Evangelicalism From Its Cultural Captivity?" *Christianity Today* 32 (August 12, 1988): 20-21. Republished as a web exclusive, September 2, 2005, www.christianitytoday.com/ct/2005/septemberweb-only/52.0.html.

[2]For a thorough academic and theological treatment, see Robert Alan Blincoe, *A New Social Contract Relating Missions Societies to Ecclesiastical Structures* (Pasadena, CA: William Carey International University, 2012).

[3]See John S. Dickerson, *The Great Evangelical Recession* (Grand Rapids: Baker, 2013) for a thorough discussion and statistical documentation.

[4]Ed Stetzer, *Lost and Found* (Nashville: Broadman & Holman, 2009), p. 1.

[5]Alan Hirsch and Tim Catchim, *The Permanent Revolution: Apostolic Imagination and Practice for the 21st Century Church* (San Francisco: Jossey-Bass, 2012), p. 247.

[6]Ibid., p. xxviii.

[7]John S. Dickerson, *The Great Evangelical Recession* (Grand Rapids: Baker Books, 2013), esp. pp. 11-120.

CHAPTER 1

[1]Ralph D. Winter, "The Two Structures of God's Redemption Mission," *Missiology* 2, no. 1 (January 1974): 121-39. Available online at http://frontiermissionfellowship.org/uploads/documents/two-structures.pdf.

[2]Kenneth Scott Latourette, *The History of Christianity*, 2 vols. (New York: Harper, 1953).

[3]The "E-scale" is a common continuum used by missiologists to illustrate cultural distance in evangelism. E-0 denotes "near-neighbor," meaning no cultural distance, while E-3 denotes significant cultural distance. See chapter three for further discussion of these concepts.

[4] George Lings, "Why Modality and Sodality Thinking Is Vital to Understand Future Church," p. 7. www.churcharmy.org.uk/Publisher/File.aspx?ID=138339 (accessed March 3, 2015).

[5]Ibid.

[6]A good commentary on the schools of the prophets is Ira M. Price, "The Schools of the Sons of the Prophets," *The Old Testament Student* 8, no. 7 (March 1889): 244-49. See www.jstor.org/stable/3156528?seq=1#page_scan _tab_contents.

[7]Johannes Blauw, *The Missionary Nature of the Church: A Survey of the Biblical Theology of Mission* (London: McGraw-Hill, 1962), pp. 55-64.

[8]Ralph D. Winter, *The Twenty-Five Unbelievable Years: 1945–1969*, 2nd ed. (Pasadena, CA: William Carey Library, 1970), p. 106.

[9]F. F. Bruce, *New Testament History* (London: Nelson, 1969), p. 78; Alfred Edersheim, *Sketches of Jewish Social Life in the Days of Christ* (London: The Religious Tract Society, 1876), p. 169.

[10]Robert Alan Blincoe, *A New Social Contract Relating Missions Structures to Ecclesiastical Structures* (Pasadena, CA: William Carey International University Press, 2012), pp. 42-52.

[11]C. Peter Wagner, *The Book of Acts: A Commentary* (Ventura, CA: Regal, 2008), p. 267.

[12]For a thorough treatment of this issue, see Joseph and Michele C., "Field-Governed Mission Structures, Part 1: In the New Testament," *International Journal of Frontier Missions* 18, no. 2 (Summer 2001): 59-66.

[13]Ibid., p. 62.

[14]Ibid., pp. 64-65.

[15]Ibid., p. 64.

[16]Wagner, *The Book of Acts: A Commentary*, p. 267.

[17]Ibid., p. 266.

[18]Craig Van Gelder, "Local and Mobile: A Study of Two Functions" (unpublished dissertation, Jackson, MS: Reformed Theological Seminary, 1975), p. 24.

[19]Charles J. Mellis, *Committed Communities: Fresh Streams for World Missions* (Pasadena, CA: William Carey Library, 1983), p. 15.

[20]Wagner, *The Book of Acts: A Commentary*, p. 266.

[21]Mellis, *Committed Communities*, p. 16. Quoting Michael Green, *Evangelism in the Early Church*, revised ed. (Grand Rapids: Eerdmans, 2003), pp. 236-37.

[22]Arthur F. Glasser, Charles Van Engen, Dean Gilliland and Shawn Redford, *Announcing the Kingdom: The Story of God's Mission in the Bible* (Grand Rapids: Baker, 2003), p. 303.

[23]Mellis, *Committed Communities*, pp. 14-16.

[24]Samuel F. Metcalf, "When Local Churches Act Like Agencies: A Fresh Look At Mission Agency-Local Church Relationships," *Evangelical Missions Quarterly* 29, no. 2 (April 1993): 142-49.

CHAPTER 2

[1]George G. Hunter III, *The Celtic Way of Evangelism: How Christianity Can Reach the West . . . Again* (Nashville: Abingdon Press, 2000); Thomas Cahill, *How the Irish Saved Civilization: The Untold Story of Ireland's Heroic Role from the Fall of Rome to the Rise of Medieval Europe* (New York: Doubleday, 1995).

[2]Sam Metcalf, "The Apostolic Through the Ages: A Cursory Summary," http://goo.gl/oRYsd1 (accessed May 6, 2015).

[3]*Annuario Pontificio* (Pontifical Yearbook), Libreria Editrice Vaticana, 2012.

[4]Winter, "Two Structures," p. 132.

[5]Kenneth Mulholland, "From Luther to Carey: Pietis and the Modern Missionary Movement," *Bibliotheca Sacra* 156, no. 1 (1999): 86.

[6]Bruce Demarest, *Satisfy Your Soul: Restoring the Heart of Christian Spirituality* (Colorado Springs, CO: Navpress, 1999), p. 29.

[7]For more on this and the Reformers' other missionary efforts, see Glenn S. Sunshine, "Protestant Missions in the Sixteenth Century," in *The Great Commission: Evangelicals and the History of World Missions*, ed. Martin I. Klauber and Scott M. Manetsch (Nashville, TN: Broadman & Holman, 2008), pp. 12-22; especially p. 14.

[8]C. Peter Wagner, *On the Crest of the Wave: Becoming a World Christian* (Ventura, CA: Regal, 1983), p. 72.

[9]See Metcalf, "The Apostolic Through the Ages," http://goo.gl/oRYsd1.

[10]Steve Addison, *Movements That Change the World: Five Keys to Spreading the Gospel* (Downers Grove, IL: InterVarsity Press, 2011), p. 22.

[11]Hunter, *The Celtic Way of Evangelism*, p. 24.

CHAPTER 3

[1]Winter, "The Two Structures of God's Redemptive Mission," p. 129.

[2]George Barna, *Revolution: Worn Out on Church? Finding Vibrant Faith Beyond the Walls of the Sanctuary* (Carol Stream, IL: Tyndale House, 2012), pp. 692-95.

[3]Mellis, *Committed Communities,* p. 5.

[4]Quoted from a conversation with Alan Hirsch (March 30, 2015).

[5]Hirsch and Catchim, *The Permanent Revolution,* p. 240.

[6]Mellis, *Committed Communities,* p. 6.

[7]Wagner, *The Book of Acts: A Commentary,* p. 345.

[8]For a more in-depth discussion of the E-scale, see Steve C. Hawthorne, *Perspectives on the World Christian Movement* (Pasadena, CA: William Carey Library, 1999), p. 64.

[9]Hirsch and Catchim, *The Permanent Revolution,* p. 208.

[10]Ibid., p. 235.

[11]George Lings, "Why Modality and Sodality Thinking Is Vital to Understand Future Church," p. 2.

[12]Hirsch and Catchim, *The Permanent Revolution,* p. 228.

[13]Barna, *Revolution,* p. 495.

[14]For more information about Re:Hope, visit rehope.co.uk.

CHAPTER 4

[1]For more information about InnerCHANGE, visit www.crmleaders.org /innerchange.

[2]Mike Breen, *The Apostle's Notebook* (Eastbourne, UK: Kingsway Publications, 2002).

[3]Hirsch and Catchim, *The Permanent Revolution.*

[4]Ibid., p. xxi.

[5]Ibid., p. xxxviii.

[6]See C. Peter Wagner, *Apostles and Prophets* (Ventura, CA: Regal, 2000), pp. 42-43.

[7]Hirsch and Catchim, *The Permanent Revolution*, p. 100.

[8]Ibid., p. 99.

[9]Hunter, *The Celtic Way of Evangelism*, p. 44.

[10]J. Robert Clinton and Richard W. Clinton, *Unlocking Your Giftedness* (Pasadena, CA: Barnabas Publishers, 1993), p. 46.

[11]Wagner, *The Book of Acts: A Commentary*, pp. 245-46, 248.

[12]Ibid., p. 346.

[13]J. Robert Clinton and Richard W. Clinton, *Unlocking Your Giftedness*, p. 145.

[14]J. Robert Clinton, *Titus: Apostolic Leadership* (Altadena, CA: Barnabas Publishing, 2001), p. 145.

[15]J. Robert Clinton, *1, 2 Timothy Commentary: Apostolic Leadership Picking up the Mantle* (Altadena, CA: Barnabas Publishers, 2006), p. 64.

[16]Adapted from J. Robert Clinton and Richard W. Clinton, *Unlocking Your Giftedness*, pp. 267-68.

[17]C. Peter Wagner, *Leading Your Church to Growth* (Grand Rapids: Regal Books, 1984), pp. 151-53.

CHAPTER 5

[1]Hirsch and Catchim, *The Permanent Revolution*, p. 16.

[2]Ibid., p. 17.

[3]Ibid., p. xix.

[4]Dick Scoggins, "Nurturing a New Generation of 'Pauline' and 'Petrine' Apostles," *Mission Frontiers* (July-August, 2006): 11-12.

[5]Hirsch and Catchim, *The Permanent Revolution*, p. 121.

[6]Ibid., p. 124.

[7]Ibid., p. 155.

[8]Adomnán of Iona, *Life of St. Columba* (London: Penguin, 1995).

CHAPTER 6

[1]Saint Benedict, *The Rule of St. Benedict in English*, ed. Timothy Fry (New York: Vintage Books, 1998), p. 10.

[2]J. Robert Clinton, *Bridging Strategies* (Pasadena, CA: Barnabas Publishers, 1992), pp. 32-37.

[3]George Lings, "Why Modality and Sodality Thinking Is Vital to Understand Future Church," p. 2.

[4]Scott Morton, *Funding Your Ministry* (Colorado Springs, CO: Dawson-Media, 2007); Steve Shadrach, *Viewpoints* (Fayetteville, AR: The Body-

Builders Press, 2009); Steve Shadrach, *The God Ask* (Fayetteville, AR: CMM Press, 2013).

[5]Michael Frost and Alan Hirsch, *The Shaping of Things to Come: Innovation and Mission for the 21st-Century Church* (Peabody, MA: Hendrickson, 2003), p. 218.

[6]See Jeri Little, *Merchant to Romania: Business as Missions in Post-Communist Eastern Europe* (Leominster, UK: Day One Publications, 2009). This is an excellent case study of business for mission.

[7]See www.stewardship.org.uk/receive-funds/toolkit-for-ministry (accessed March 26, 2015).

[8]Henri J. M. Nouwen, *A Spirituality of Fundraising* (Nashville, TN: Upper Room Books, 2011), p. 15.

[9]Robert E. Coleman, *The Master Plan of Evangelism* (Grand Rapids: Revell, 1963), pp. 32, 33.

[10]Available from CRM (July 2014), http://goo.gl/DkVQuz.

[11]Libby Little, address at Urbana Student Missions Conference, December 1996.

CHAPTER 7

[1]J. Robert Clinton, *1 and 2 Timothy: Apostolic Leadership: Picking up the Mantle*, Clinton's Biblical Leadership Commentary Series (Pasadena, CA: Barnabas Publishers, 2006), pp. 171-76.

[2]Ralph Winter, "Editorial Comment," *Mission Frontiers* (March-April 2003): 4-5.

[3]J. Robert Clinton, *1 and 2 Timothy*, pp. 171-76.

[4]Warren Bennis, *Managing People Is Like Herding Cats: Warren Bennis on Leadership* (Provo, UT: Executive Excellence Publishing, 1999), p. 21.

[5]Quoted in "The Critical Issue is Leadership," *Net Fax: Leadership Network* 50 (July 22, 1996): 1.

[6]Here I'm drawing on the ideas of Lindley Baldwin, *Samuel Morris* (Bloomington, MN: Bethany House Publishers, 1987), pp. 77-78.

[7]Coleman, *The Master Plan of Evangelism*, pp. 33, 32.

[8]J. Robert Clinton, *Teaching as a Career: How to Develop Yourself for an Effective Ministry* (Altadena, CA: Barnabas Publishers, 2000), p. 40.

[9]Andre Millard, "Machine Shop Culture and Menlo Park," in *Working At Inventing: Thomas A. Edison and the Menlo Park Experience*, ed. by William S. Pretzer (Baltimore: The Johns Hopkins University Press, 2002), p. 56.

[10]J. Robert Clinton, "Two Important Macro Lessons," lecture at Fuller Theological Seminary.

[11]John 1:35-51 is an excellent case study in such situational recruiting.

[12]Betty Lee Skinner, *Daws: The Biography of Dawson Trotman, Founder of the Navigators* (Grand Rapids: Zondervan, 1974), p. 82.

[13]Coleman, *The Master Plan of Evangelism*, pp. 21, 126.

[14]Joseph Bayly, "In Celebration of Missionaries," in *Psalms of My Life* (Colorado Springs, CO: David C. Cook, 1987), p. 82-83.

CHAPTER 8

[1]Metcalf, "When Local Churches Act Like Agencies" (see chap. 1, note 20).

[2]Wagner, *Leading Your Church to Growth*, pp. 149-50.

[3]ECFA Church Pulse, January 2015. www.ecfa.org/Pulse/Church/2015/Church Pulse_M01_2015.pdf.

[4]Consultative Group on International Agricultural Research, www.cgiar .org/consortium-news/postharvest-loss-reduction-a-significant-focus -of-cgiar-research.

[5]Hartford Institute for Religion Research, http://hirr.hartsem.edu/mega church/definition.html (accessed May 8, 2015).

[6]Frost and Hirsch, *The Shaping of Things to Come*, p. 147.

[7]John Dickerson, *The Great Evangelical Recession* (Grand Rapids: Baker Books, 2013), p. 84.

[8]Ibid., pp. 84-94.

[9]Hirsch and Catchim, *The Permanent Revolution*, p. 247.

[10]An article that I've found very helpful for local churches struggling with the recruiting, development and sending of people from their bodies to serve in sodalities is "What Is a Church to Do? The Dilemma of Missionary Funding in a Changing World." It is available from CRM at http:// goo.gl/4dPoFh.

[11]Linda Monckton, "Churches and Closure in the Church of England: A Summary Report," March 2010, www.docin.com/p-780889146.html.

[12]Soeren Kern, "Muslims Converting Empty European Churches into Mosques," January 16, 2012, www.gatestoneinstitute.org/2761/converting -churches-into-mosques.

[13]"Redundant Churches: Pints in the Pews," *The Economist*, March 28, 2002, www.economist.com/node/1057312.

[14]Winter, *The Two Structures of God's Redemptive Mission*, pp. 128-29.

CHAPTER 9

[1]Douglas Hyde, *Dedication and Leadership: Learning From the Communists* (Notre Dame, IN: University of Notre Dame Press, 1966); Stephane Courtois, Nicolas Werth, Jean-Louis Panne, Andrzej Paczkowski, Karel Bartosek and Jean-Louis Margolin, *The Black Book of Communism: Crimes, Terror, Repression* (Cambridge, MA: The Presidents and Fellows of Harvard College, 1999), p. 4.

[2]Hyde, *Dedication and Leadership*, p. 35.

[3]Alexander Balmain Bruce, *The Training of the Twelve; or, Passages Out of the Gospels Exhibiting the Twelve Disciples of Jesus Under Discipline for the Apostleship* (Grand Rapids: Kregel Publications, 1971).

[4]Coleman, *Master Plan of Evangelism* (see chap. 6, note 10).

[5]Ibid., p. 18.

[6]Addison, *Movements That Change the World* (see chap. 2, note 9).

[7]Steve Addison, *What Jesus Started: Joining the Movement, Changing the World* (Downers Grove, IL: InterVarsity Press, 2012).

[8]Trevor Yaxley and Carolyn Vanderwal, *William and Catherine: The Life and Legacy of the Booths, Founders of the Salvation Army: A New Biography* (Minneapolis: Bethany House, 2003), p. 145.

[9]Ibid., p. 147.

[10]J. Oswald Sanders, *Spiritual Leadership* (Chicago: Moody Press, 1967), pp. 127-28.

[11]Yaxley and Vanderwal, *William and Catherine*, p. 145.

[12]John Reed, *Ten Days That Shook the World* (London: Penguin, 2007).

[13]Henry David Thoreau, *Walden* (New York: Thomas Y. Crowell, 1910), p. 8.

[14]Oliver Wendell Holmes, *The Poems of Oliver Wendell Holmes* (New York: Thomas Y. Crowell, 1955), p. 430.

[15]J. Edwin Orr, *The Fervent Prayer* (Chicago: Moody Press, 1974).

[16]Ibid., pp. 96-97.

[17]Charles Moore, *Daniel H. Burnham, Architect, Planner of Cities* (Boston: Houghton Mifflin, 1921), p. 1921.

[18]Floyd McClung, "What Is Apostolic Passion?," July 26, 2013, www .ywamheidebeek.org/what-is-apostolic-passion-by-floyd-mcclung.

[19]Matt Rawlins, "Expectations" (January, 2008). www.ywamdtscentre.com /ywamers/matt/Jan08%20Vol10.83.htm.

[20]Alan Hirsch, *The Forgotten Ways: Reactivating the Missional Church*

(Grand Rapids: Brazos, 2009), p. 144.

[21]Donald A. McGavran, *Understanding Church Growth* (Grand Rapids: Eerdmans, 1990), p. 204.

[22]Ibid., p. 207.

[23]Tom Peters, *Thriving on Chaos: Handbook for a Management Revolution* (New York: Knopf, 1987), p. 659.

[24]Ibid., p. 56.

[25]Ibid., p. 666.

[26]James C. Galvin, "Avoiding the Downside of Excellence," *Excelerate* 4 (2012): 5-6. http://galvinandassociates.com/wordpress_site/wp-content /uploads/2012/11/Avoiding-the-Downside-of-Excellence.pdf.

[27]Peters, *Thriving on Chaos*, p. 4.

[28]Hirsch and Frost, *The Shaping of Things to Come*, p. 142 (see chap. 6, note 6).

[29]Hirsch, *The Forgotten Ways*, p. 113.

[30]Addison, *Movements That Change the World*, p. 117.

[31]Clinton was professor of leadership at the School of Intercultural Studies at Fuller Theological Seminary until his retirement in 2010. He wrote a number of books and pioneered the application of the concepts of leadership emergence theory to the way God develops and forms leaders over a lifetime.

[32]Dean M. Kelley, *Why Conservative Churches Are Growing: A Study in Sociology of Religion* (Macon, GA: Mercer University Press, 1995).

[33]David Brooks, "Creed or Chaos," *New York Times*, April 22, 2011.

[34]Dietrich Bonhoeffer, *The Cost of Discipleship* (New York: Touchstone, 1995), p. 89.

[35]Addison, *Movements That Change the World*, p. 64.

[36]Ibid.

[37]Metcalf, "The Apostolic Through the Ages," http://goo.gl/oRYsd1 (accessed May 8, 2015).

CHAPTER 10

[1]http://www.accelerateteams.org.

[2]Jerry Trousdale, *Miraculous Movements: How Hundreds of Thousands of Muslims Are Falling in Love with Jesus* (Nashville: Thomas Nelson, 2012).

[3]Patrick Robertson and David Watson with Gregory C. Benoit, *The Father Glorified: True Stories of God's Power Through Ordinary People* (Nashville: Thomas Nelson, 2013).

[4]See Roy Moran, *Spent Matches: Igniting the Signal Fire for the Spiritually Dissatisfied* (Nashville: Thomas Nelson, 2015). The chapter entitled "The Hybrid Church" offers an excellent explanation of how to integrate Accelerate's processes and philosophy of ministry in a local church context.

[5]There are two foundational concepts in Accelerate: (1) The discovery process using the Bible (often orally), and (2) finding and cultivating persons of peace and seeing these discovery groups (most often recruited and led by persons of peace) multiply through their social relationships.

The term "persons of peace" comes directly from Matthew 10, Luke 9, Luke 10 and Mark 6. These are the four passages where Jesus sends out the disciples two-by-two (the Twelve in three of the passages and the Seventy in Luke 10). The result of their ministry of proclaiming the kingdom, healing the sick, driving out demons and raising the dead was to identify "persons of peace." These were the people who were responsive to the truth, whom God had prepared beforehand. They were foundational to the spread of the good news of Jesus in their communities.

[6]Winter, *The Two Structures of God's Redemptive Mission*, p. 24.

[7]Ori Brafman and Rod A. Beckstrom, *The Starfish and the Spider: The Unstoppable Power of Leaderless Organizations* (New York: Portfolio, 2006).

[8]John B. Hayes, director of InnerCHANGE, has written about this order in his book, *Sub-merge: Living Deep in a Shallow World: Service, Justice and Contemplation Among the World's Poor* (Ventura, CA: Regal Books, 2006).

[9]For more information about neo-monastic movements, see Scott Bessenecker, *The New Friars: The Emerging Movement Serving the World's Poor* (Downers Grove, IL: InterVarsity Press, 2006).

[10]Pew Research Center Religion and Public Life Project, "Global Christianity— A Report on the Size and Distribution of the World's Christian Population," December 19, 2011, www.pewforum.org/2011/12/19/global-christianity -exec.

CONCLUSION

[1]John Piper, *Let the Nations Be Glad* (Grand Rapids: Baker Books, 1993), p. 15.

About the Author

Sam Metcalf is the president of CRM (Church Resource Ministries).

He holds a BA with honors from the University of Virginia and earned a masters degree from the School of Intercultural Studies at Fuller Theological Seminary and a DMin from the Fuller School of Theology.

He worked in international sales and marketing with Read Steel/ Read International in Birmingham, Alabama, before serving in Southern California as a staff representative of the Navigators. In 1980 he was one of the original founders of CRM and assumed responsibility as president in 1985. He is ordained in the Evangelical Free Church of America.

Sam is responsible for the spiritual vitality and effectiveness of CRM teams and personnel who serve throughout the world. He also coordinates CoNext, an international partnership of likeminded apostolic organizations in a growing number of nations. These responsibilities require travel and firsthand work in a variety of overseas and crosscultural contexts.

His wife, Patty, is an active partner in ministry and focuses her gifts and efforts on healing prayer and helping others grow in intimacy with God. When possible, Patty travels with Sam and they minister together among CRM staff worldwide. The Metcalfs have two married children and four grandchildren.

CRM EMPOWERING LEADERS

Church Resource Ministries (CRM)—the organization that the author leads—works to create movements of committed followers of Jesus throughout the world.

In all of their ministry environments, CRM personnel pursue spiritual depth and innovative strategies that

Pioneer new ground among the unreached, unchurched and dechurched,

Bring lasting transformation among the poor, and

Mobilize the church for mission.

Over five hundred full-time CRM staff creatively implement these three initiatives in a variety of cultures and contexts in over eighty nations, including many difficult—and sometimes dangerous—places among people far from God.

CRM also provides training for thousands of pastors, church leaders and church planters in partnership with over fifty different denominations throughout North America.

For more information, visit crmleaders.org.

267
M 5885

LINCOLN CHRISTIAN UNIVERSITY   i30897

3 4711 00225 8541